PRIMARY CARE

PRIMARY CARE

A Doctor's Life North and South of the Border

Emily Hartzog, MD

SANTA FE

Sunstone books may be purchased for educational, business, or sales promotional use.
For information please write: Special Markets Department, Sunstone Press,
P.O. Box 2321, Santa Fe, New Mexico 87504-2321.

Book and Cover design › Vicki Ahl
Body typeface › Perpetua
Printed on acid-free paper

Library of Congress Cataloging-in-Publication Data

Hartzog, Emily, 1958-
  Primary care : a doctor's life north and south of the border / by Emily Hartzog.
    p. ; cm.
  ISBN 978-0-86534-934-6 (softcover : alk. paper)
  I. Title.
  [DNLM: 1. Hartzog, Emily, 1958- 2. Physicians--Mexico--Autobiography. 3. Physicians-
-United States--Autobiography. 4. Community Health Services--Mexico. 5. Community
Health Services--United States. 6. Health Services, Indigenous--Mexico. 7. Health Services,
Indigenous--United States. 8. Primary Health Care--Mexico. 9. Primary Health Care-
-United States. WZ 100]

  610.92--dc23
  [B]
                            2012050466

WWW.SUNSTONEPRESS.COM
SUNSTONE PRESS / POST OFFICE BOX 2321 / SANTA FE, NM 87504-2321 /USA
(505) 988-4418 / ORDERS ONLY (800) 243-5644 / FAX (505) 988-1025

1

I EMERGED FROM THE HOSPITAL STAIRWELL, my pockets laden with syringes, needles, and blood tubes. My short white coat marked me as a medical student, and I clinked as I walked past the patients lined up in the hallway waiting to be admitted. The fluorescent lights and industrial green paint of the Charleston V.A. made even the healthier patients look sick. I recognized the one I was looking for on the second gurney down from the Emergency Room door.

Before I got started, the attending physician took me on one side in a conspiratorial manner and said, "Mr. James has been a teaching case long enough."

I wondered what this could possibly mean. I had admitted Mr. James for a similar problem less than a month ago when he had heavy bleeding from his esophagus as a result of chronic alcoholism. He had tolerated the nasogastric tube that I pushed down his nose and throat without flinching. Afterwards, as I pumped large syringes of ice water down the tube to try to control his bleeding, he had splattered less of the sickly alcoholic vomit on my plastic apron than usual. I remembered most vividly the kindness of his smile.

"A teaching case?" I fished for clues.

"He has been a perfect example of the effects of chronic alcohol abuse for lots of medical students like you, but we've given him more than his share of the blood supply." The pressure of the attending's hand on the sleeve of my white coat became unbearable. He leaned over and whispered, "No more blood for Mr. James," then sauntered away.

I stood frozen in the nurses' station. I tried to fathom how we could refuse to transfuse a patient and let him bleed to death, when it would be so easy to save him. I ran to find the resident on duty, who confirmed my worst fears and added that I was the one who should give Mr. James the news.

I huddled over the chart at some distance in the hallway feeling exposed by the bright lights. I wondered how to tell him we were going to let him die when help was right here in the building; it was too awful to even say out loud. I found myself edging forward. He looked sheepish and guilty when he saw me; his face was as pale as the beige print hospital gown tied behind his neck. The other patients in the hall watched like bored cows in a field.

"Mr. James, they've decided not to give you blood this time."

He made no response. I stood in front of him trying not to cry.

"We'll keep giving you IV fluids which should make you comfortable."

He took my hand, gave it a squeeze, and flashed his kind smile. He was more concerned with my discomfort than his own demise.

I knew that if he were 'Charleston Society', we would already have blood running in one arm and, in the other, medicinal alcohol mixed with intravenous fluids so he wouldn't go through withdrawal. But Mr. James was just a poor veteran from John's Island who had no one left who cared about him. My pleas for his life, coming as they did from a lowly medical student and woman, fell on deaf ears.

In the previous three years of medical school, I had dutifully performed all the heart-rending tasks demanded of me to get to the pot at the end of the rainbow. I guillotined rats in deep sinks that I had held, fed, and injected daily for months. I decapitated wriggling frogs with scissors to watch them swim headless in tanks leaving bloody trails behind them. I cut the hearts out of big beautiful turtles to observe how long they beat afterwards in petri dishes. And I anesthetized and operated on trusting dogs who were destroyed at the end of the procedure. Causing more sorrow was definitely not the bright future I had envisioned.

2

I SPENT THE FOURTH AND FINAL YEAR of medical school in South Carolina planning my escape. My last eight years had been spent in Charleston at an antebellum college and the medical university, and I had steeped in the South for long enough. I couldn't wait to move to New York City for my residency training and never really considered going anywhere else.

The weather was balmy on Valentine's Day of that last year. I stopped by the grocery store after I finished my work at the hospital and heard the wind rustle the palmettos as I walked up the wooden ramp. I stared at the food from the center of the aisles and contemplated buying a steak and a bottle of wine to celebrate on my own, but I lost heart and left with only a bunch of multi-colored Gladioli.

I put them in a vase on the coffee table of my carriage house apartment and settled down on the sofa with a book. I decided not to worry about dinner until I was hungry and felt relieved when the phone rang a couple of hours later. I found myself agreeing to a date with someone whom I had turned down many times before, but it was at my favorite restaurant in Charleston. The chef was a Sikh from India, and their aromatic kitchen always made me want everything on the menu. He said we were going to be having dinner with the owner. I realized in all the years I had been going there, I had never met him before.

Soon after the two of us arrived, John, the owner, joined us at the table. He was forty years old, with a soft English accent, a sharp intellect, and an easy smile. The two of us quickly turned to a discussion about health care in England and America.

I said, "It may not be obvious, but people get radically different care at the veterans' hospitals and the private ones. Our system has a safety net, but the wealthy have many more options than the poor."

"After the rich and poor fought together in the wars, England decided to provide healthcare to everyone as an equal right. You can't ration health when people are willing to die for their country." John was a passionate supporter of the N.H.S.

"I would love to work with the National Health Service and see what it's like." I bit into a samosa with fragrant potatoes and peas inside.

"Well, it's not without its flaws, you know, but it's vital; and most of the time, it gets the job done. Let me know if you're interested and have the time. I may be able to come up with some connections."

"I am interested, but I may not have the time. I'm planning to move to New York City for my Ob/Gyn residency this summer." He looked at me a little too long; I blushed and tried to pay more attention to my date.

As the evening progressed, I became more and more fascinated with John. He joked about polo games, told stories of life in Britain, and treated his staff with considerable respect. When we finally caught up with each other again some months later, it felt as if we belonged together.

My sister, Callie was quick to warn me of his escapades with policemen and women. She was eight years older and knew him from the restaurants and the people she hung out with. She told me he flirted shamelessly, especially with young women, and never hesitated to throw a punch even if he decked someone across one of his own tables.

I thought he was perfect. He was the ultimate romantic. He sketched portraits of me on napkins and wrote me poetry. He made elaborate meals for me at his house in the country and took me to meet his polo ponies. He was a mixture of opposites; boyish and sophisticated, intellectual and ridiculous, charming and vulnerable. And he didn't sweat the details of life.

He drove a Mercedes, and his Golden Retriever went everywhere with him. She spent as much time on his back seat as she did at his house, and we poured her dog food directly onto the leather upholstery. He had many guests to his beautiful cabin in the pinewoods outside Charleston and was delighted to add the clothes that anyone left behind to his limited wardrobe.

He would suddenly decide to buy Gucci loafers, then be nonplussed when none of his credit cards worked.

We could get out of the ocean, put rumpled jeans over wet bathing suits, and be fussed over at any Charleston restaurant. We even got pulled over by the cops for expired license plates, with open beers in the cup holders, and John got away with having no valid driver's license or registration.

There was a fifteen year age difference between us; we came from two different generations and two different worlds. I wanted to live in New York; he owned three restaurants in Charleston and had no desire to live in the city. And my time left in Charleston was short. The obstacles prompted us to decide to marry in less than a month.

My parents had been patiently waiting for me to find someone I was interested in, but panicked when I asked them to make the trip down to meet him. My mother quickly deemed him the most charming man she had ever met, but said it with a sneer that increased with each reiteration.

My whole family felt so strongly about me making a big mistake that they united in an intervention staged at a beach house one afternoon when John was busy with the restaurants in town. My sister and mother led the discussion which focused mainly on how manipulative and calculating John could be. I thought a pleasant day had simply taken a bad turn until my brother and father chimed in. As the youngest, I listened angrily and contributed little. And then I went right ahead with my plans.

We were married later that same year by an auto mechanic with two witnesses in a ceremony that took ten minutes and cost twenty dollars. My family sent no presents because they weren't invited.

There was no possibility of us living together for the first four years of the marriage. John wrote weekly love letters on beautiful stationery and came to New York once or twice a month. I worked, caught up on sleep when I wasn't working, and looked forward to the time we spent together. John's life in Charleston still included many late nights with drinking and dancing. I decided not to let it worry me and concentrated on surviving the training instead.

I got my wish, and we moved to England after I finished my residency in 1988. I took exams in London, registered as a foreign doctor, and interviewed in several small hospitals before taking a job in rural Somerset. John had sold all his restaurants, but one, and had a reliable partner. He was eager to move home and write the novel he had been thinking about for so long.

We wanted lots of children, and I had tried to get pregnant as early as the second year in New York. Soon after the move to England, we found out that it wasn't going to be possible for me to have John's children, so I gave up trying. John was devastated and made more than a few people uncomfortable by being too quick to announce that it was his problem and not mine. I accepted it as fate and did my best not to show any disappointment to spare him any feelings of guilt.

The National Health Service was at one of its peaks of inefficiency while I was working in England, and I was shocked at the amount of time it took to become a Consultant. I found a brochure in the drawer of a call room nightstand that said the average age was forty-two. John worked hard on a novel, but couldn't find a publisher when he was finished.

I was in the Somerset library one day flipping through an American journal and found an advertisement for a job working with the Indian Health Service. When I told John about it that night, he was more than eager to make the move, so I flew back and interviewed in Tuba City, Shiprock, and Chinle. I decided to take the job in Shiprock.

We stayed not quite two years in England overall. We felt confined by all parameters of our life in Britain; the boundaries there were much too well-defined. We had more expansive notions of what life could be like and enough energy to keep searching; wherever it might take us.

The Indian Health Service was America's biggest system of public health, and John and I had a memorable vacation visiting a cousin of mine who taught in Tuba City a few years before. We moved back to America in the summer of 1990 with only our suitcases. We were both excited to start life in the Navajo Nation; a country within our country.

3

THE ROAD FROM BLUFF, UTAH WAS DWARFED by blood red cliffs, which changed to pink sandstone as we approached Colorado. The state line also marked the boundary of the Navajo Reservation, so the hogans and shade houses gave way to corrals and barns. A mountain range sprung up close-by to the south and became more dominant as we progressed. It felt cooler in the July heat under its green shadow.

John and I were returning from a camping trip in Canyonlands in Utah. We had four dogs in the car, and I smelled worse than they did, having not had a shower in three days.

A Choctaw physician at work named Owen had told me to take this route home. "This road is amazing. Owen said it had everything…mountains, canyons, creeks, Indian ruins. He never goes anywhere else."

"These look like proper working ranches." John said and nodded in approval.

"There's where he said you could park to hike." I pointed through the open car window.

We pulled onto a huge expanse of stone with a lonely sign-in box in the middle of it. I let the dogs out of the car, and they explored the pink sand around the edges covered in desert sage, driftwood, and bits of cactus.

"Look at those alfalfa fields under the Ute Mountain. Wouldn't that be the perfect place to live?" I couldn't stop staring at the farm across the street.

"Pretty perfect. They could be polo fields." John couldn't take his eyes off it either.

We walked up to the rock formations above where we parked and found an Anasazi wall over our heads built in a corridor between two of them. Feeling too tired to go any further, we called the dogs, and they leapt back into the Honda Acura.

A small trailer sat at the front of the farm across the street with an enormous garden beside it. Vegetables and fruit were laid out across hay bales beside a chalkboard with a list and prices. We decided to go and look at them for dinner because there wasn't a grocery store for miles and our refrigerator was empty. The dogs hung out the car windows and panted as we parked in front of the sign under the shade of an open-sided hay barn.

"Peaches sound pretty delicious right now, and we could make a fresh sauce for pasta with the tomatoes and have cantaloupe for dessert. Wait, it says the farm is for sale by owner in smaller writing at the bottom." John sounded dangerously excited.

"John, let's come back to discuss that. The dogs are all thirsty, we're filthy and smell like a campfire, and I'm dying for some food that doesn't have sand in it."

"Just let me ask."

"You can ask, but we can't stay."

John got out and knocked at the door of the trailer. An old cowboy came out, and they walked over to the hay barn and looked at tomatoes. They talked and talked. I could feel drops of drool from one of the dogs in the back seat hitting my shoulder.

John came back over to the car, "He said we could let the dogs out."

"I hope they're okay with his sheep."

"They're reservation mutts, remember?"

I let them out. They touched noses with a couple of ewes then quickly lost interest. The cowboy's name was Gene. He was polite and had an old-fashioned way of talking; everything was preceded by 'a man might could do this:'. His tomatoes and melons were flawless.

We stood on a small hillock behind the sheep pens, and he pointed out the edges of his property; eighty acres in total that stretched eastward to a line of cottonwood trees at the edge of the alfalfa fields. To the south, the property crossed a creek and reached up to the first shelf of the mountain. A mesa ending in a cliff faced his western side. The line to the north was the road.

Gene said, "We're the number one ditch." Neither John nor I had any idea what this meant, but Gene seemed to think it was important.

"How many cuts of hay do you get off the fields?" John knew so much more about farming than I did. I didn't know you cut more than once a season.

"A man can get four if he's lucky and can count on three the other years."

"And why are you selling it?"

"I wouldn't sell it, but Dolores wants to move closer to the grandkids in town, and we aren't getting any younger."

"How about if we bought it and you taught me how to farm it for the first two years and took the profit and subtracted it from the asking price. That way you'd get to stay a little longer, we'd get a little off the top, and I'd know what I was doing when I took it over."

Gene grinned from ear to ear, "That sure sounds like a good plan to me." They shook hands, and we piled back in the car with tomatoes, peaches, a watermelon, and a cantaloupe.

I looked at John in disbelief and said, "I think we just bought a farm."

It was 1992, and we had lived in a dusty compound on the reservation in Shiprock for two years. We looked at a couple of pieces of land for sale near the borders in New Mexico and Colorado, but not with any serious intent. John was currently in the middle of writing a second novel, and I liked my work at the hospital. We were both certain that we wanted to stay close-by, so maybe it was the right time to make a commitment. Maybe it would always feel terrifying whether it was the right time or not.

4

WE WERE THE FIRST NEWCOMERS to McElmo in quite a while, and the first, in even longer, to settle fourteen miles down the canyon road. We took a picnic to the eroded sandbank, where we wanted to build the house, right after we bought the property. We were so excited to be eating apples from one of our own trees nearby. We built a small fire with brushwood and cooked bratwurst to go with them.

The project looked daunting on the day of our picnic. I had never contemplated living somewhere that was in the middle of nowhere before. Our carefully selected site for the house was above McElmo Creek at the bottom of the property. You could hear it flowing from anywhere you stood on the sandbank. The Sleeping Ute Mountain stretched out end to end in the form of a reclining brave, and a gentle peak that formed his hair was the part the house was going to be facing. The sun had gone down behind the cliff called the Battlerock at the edge of the mesa that dominated the west. It cast its shadow across us and the impossibly green alfalfa fields on the other side.

"This is a long way from the main road, and the road from Gene's is pretty rough. Will that be a problem?"

"No, Gene says there's another way in from the road under the Battlerock."

"And how will we get electricity and plumbing down here? And what about water?"

"We'll have to bring the electric wires down from the road and put in a couple of poles. We'll figure out where we want the septic tank and leach field; over there maybe." John pointed towards the apple tree. "And then we'll need to dig a well. Gene says he's great at witching water. He's got a stick up at the trailer that he always uses."

"It's a split stick, and you hold the forked end in your hands and it vibrates when it's over water, right? Don't let him do it until I'm around. I can't wait to see that."

"I'll tell him he'll have an audience. I think it would suit him just fine." John smiled at the thought.

"Who's going to build the house?"

"Hal knows a couple of firemen in Farmington who are contractors, and he says they're really good guys. I'm supposed to meet them next week."

"How long do you think it'll take? A year?"

"Nah, I think we'll do it quicker than that."

Very soon afterwards, we were in the middle of a right of way dispute. Our neighbor to the south, Betty Porter, was a crusty ranch woman of seventy-five who had raised her family on a large farm that was further down the road under the Battlerock. We knew it wasn't a good sign when, right after we bought the property, she invited John down for iced tea to let him know that she didn't like newcomers and was going to do everything in her power to make it difficult for us to stay. Now, she had a mission.

The dirt track to the west, which Gene pointed out to John as a way into the property, was on higher ground and came off a good road by the Battlerock. This was a relief because the rutted road from Gene's trailer to the creek was more suitable for his tractor than our car. We thought the Battlerock road was a Bureau of Land Management right of way because the Battlerock was BLM land. In fact, the track under dispute crossed another trapped piece of BLM land next to our western border, but we thought they would acknowledge it as a way through. Betty argued that she had paid fifty years ago for the right of way on the Battlerock road; and within days of us using it, she had the sheriff parked at the top of the road and informed us that we had no easement.

In the meantime, we hired a local construction crew made up of volunteer firemen and started the groundwork for construction. Only a few days after the sheriff's visit, Betty blocked their progress with a gate draped with heavy chains at the entrance. Like most of the locals, she loved nothing better than a fight. The more we used the road down from the Gene's trailer, the worse it got.

We called the sheriff to come back on our behalf, but he refused. John made multiple visits to the BLM office in Durango and was told that they would begin an investigation of the Battlerock road, but it would probably take several months. They also said we could apply to buy the trapped piece of land to our west, and it might come through in time to benefit our grandchildren.

Betty remained angry and unapproachable. We found out that a hundred years ago, an angry group of Constitutionalists had congregated in McElmo Canyon. They rode into town in an armed posse, arrested the mayor and sheriff, and put them in a make-shift jail on the creek-bank for a few days. As the modern-day canyon controversy increased, John became more and more convinced that he had found the place where he belonged.

He matched Betty play by play in the right of way dispute. When she said the road looked like it had never been used, he had Gene ride over and over it with the tractor and plant wild grass mix on the sides. When she was spotted going to see the sheriff in town, he quickly followed suit. I was worried about her jumping out from behind a bush, freshly-permed with a pistol, every time I went to see the progress on the house.

The climax came one day when a cement truck got stuck, and we desperately needed to get the other one through Betty's entrance, which still looked like the entrance to Fort Knox. Our contractor decided to dig out the post to dismantle her gate, and we got both trucks through before the cement hardened. He dutifully put it all back up following, but she got wind of the incident from her son Mike.

A few nights afterwards, she pulled up to the contractor's house in a dress, stockings, and sensible shoes. She unloaded some tools from her car, knelt down, and began to take apart his gate. When he asked her what she was doing, she said that she wanted him to see what it felt like to have your property invaded. When he said his dog could be really fierce, she said he'd better put the dog inside or she'd shoot it.

He called us and quit the job the next day. Fortunately we had two contractors, so the other one took over. Gene told us not to take her too seriously because she'd always been ornery; ornery was an understatement.

It was years before the whole thing was resolved. Betty moved to town, but still came down to argue every time a meeting was called. Whole teams of archeologists, Bureau of Land Management officials, and lawyers were enlisted at various junctures. We ended up paying a nominal fee to her for the easement.

It was hard to imagine why she'd gone to all the trouble until it was over and John admitted that Gene confided to him, early on, that the track hadn't been used more than a few times before we came. When I asked how both of them carried on with such conviction, he said, "We got what we wanted, didn't we?"

5

THE YEAR WE BUILT OUR HOUSE was fraught with flooding. The Bureau of Land Management and archeologists had to approve digging the holes to place the power poles, and we didn't want to wait, so the crew did the entire construction project with generator power in the mud. Fortunately, they were a good-natured bunch and as resourceful as true homesteaders.

I had argued for a miner's cabin, but we built two houses; a one bedroom guest house, which resembled a Dove Creek pinto bean silo with a corrugated tin roof and ours, a territorial house, with garret windows and tapering sides, which nestled beside it. The earth was gathered to create a mountain of dirt and sand, and we put a cement monolithic slab on top to give the houses stability because of the nearness to the creek. The crew found building the four identical floors of the guest tower an interesting challenge until it came time to install the two story windows in the rain. Our house was simpler, but slanting the sides and constructing the grids for the wine-colored cement floors were things they had never done before either. John camped on the property during most of that year; so between all of them, they figured it out quickly.

The monumental rainstorm happened when John was away and the houses were almost completed. I panicked and drove up from Shiprock, where I was still living, the next day after I finished work. McElmo Creek had turned into a roaring river; and as I progressed down the canyon, every bend in the road brought new versions of destruction. When I got to Gene's trailer at the top of the property, the noise of the water was deafening even though it was a quarter mile from the creek. Gene and Dolores weren't home, so I decided to walk rather than drive to the bottom because it felt safer.

The churning muddy torrent surrounded our new sand hill with hundred year old cottonwoods turning over end to end and boulders as big as cars carried along in the fray. But the houses stood solid, and the water lines showed that the flood was receding. In spite of my relief, I still felt afraid and only relaxed when I turned off the canyon road and the noise of the creek finally stopped.

My anxieties were all magnified by worrying about money. The sale of the last of John's restaurants had helped with the down payment to purchase the farm, but my salary in Shiprock was barely enough to cover the note on our construction costs much less any living expenses. John was going to continue to write full-time, so he wasn't going to be working, and I had no way to increase my income. I convinced myself that we could live on nothing, but it nagged me in my sleep.

John had flown to Charleston when the big rains came. The plan was for him to return by driving a U-Haul truck across the country loaded with the remainder of our furniture from the South. I decided to go back to McElmo Canyon over the weekend to look at the dirt roads and gauge when they would be dry enough to get the truck to the houses at the bottom.

When I arrived at the turning to the farm from the main road at the top, I could no longer hear the roaring of the creek through the open windows of my Toyota pick-up. Betty's road was still locked up solid, and the road that led down from Gene's place to the houses was wrecked by the combination of the crew's trucks and the rain. The ruts were so deep that I had to drive in the alfalfa field for more than half the way, and I winced as I heard my tires permanently crushing part of the year's crop.

It was a Sunday, so there was no one at the construction site. I parked on a mound of dry ground in the back and pulled on rubber boots. My boots gathered so much mud on them that it was hard to lift my feet as I went over to check on the creek. There was still shallow water eddying around what was normally dry ground at the bottom, but the flood waters had stayed at a safe distance throughout. I decided not to peek in the camp trailer in the back, where John had been living during the construction, because it was in the middle of a puddle.

I walked in the mud around the outside of the houses and looked in the windows. The tower had hundreds of nails in the dirt around its periphery and looked impossibly tall and incongruous. I heard some locals had already named it Fort Battlerock. I figured the mustard yellow stucco on the main house must have been a topic of conversation in town for weeks.

I stood on the red and white cement tiles that checkered the porch and gazed at the creek, It was the color of milky coffee, and I could smell the sand churning in the water. The land around looked wild and vast. I couldn't believe I actually owned so much of it. Our rental house on the compound in Shiprock was feeling smaller and smaller, and it wasn't helped by the fact that we had sold or moved all of the furniture except a bed and a chair.

For a month, I had been sleeping in the bed and moving the chair to where I needed it most. It was a bedside table at night, a place for folded clothes during the day, and could be pulled up to the windowsill in the main room which doubled as a table for meals. The dogs hadn't been out of the chain-link fence in the back for weeks. We were all ready to move, but the road was so bad that I decided to put John off from leaving for a couple of days. I sincerely hoped it wouldn't rain again in the meantime.

I slipped off my boots and walked inside the house. The sound echoed from the door when I closed it. The pieces of furniture that we had moved in from Shiprock looked dwarfed and lonely, but the house was already beautiful inside without much of anything in it. The colors were out of the box of crayons that created McElmo's red and yellow canyons and the raised adobe fireplace looked cozy in front of the far window that was filled with the sheer wall of the Battlerock outside.

It felt so different to be walking around the empty house on my own. I looked at the different rooms and could picture us having breakfast and sitting in front of the fire; but, at the same time, a part of me wanted to have it all to myself. I realized that this was probably going to be the last time I would feel that this house was mine and mine alone. It was the last time that I would be selfish enough to say it, even to myself; and it was the last time the rooms would contain only my presence. In the future, my beautiful house and awe-inspiring farm would be filled with other people and other things. I bade them hello and goodbye in the same day.

6

'OLD GENE TOZER', who was only in his early seventies, was a big part of our lives in the early days. His family was one of the first to homestead in the Cortez area, and he had lived on the land that he sold to us for at least thirty years. He was small and wiry with a bowlegged cowboy gait, and he'd lost part of one lung in surgery, so he kept slightly bent to that side. He was the master of tall tales; and his big brown eyes, accentuated by thick granny glasses, helped him seem all the more convincing. His wife Dolores tried, in vain, to keep him in line.

"When I was in the service, Judy Garland came and did a show for us. She picked me out of the crowd and said, 'Come here, Cowboy.' She wanted to take me home with her, but I had to turn her down. Do you remember that Dolores?"

"No, I wasn't there, Gene!"

"She wrote to me afterwards and said she'd never forget me. Do you remember where I put that letter?"

"No Gene, I never saw the letter."

"I know I have it here somewhere, I'm sure I kept it."

"Well, you never showed it to me."

One afternoon, we had Gene and Dolores to our newly finished house for lunch and were sitting in the sun that streamed through the dining room windows. Gene started reminiscing about the time that he and Dolores found a newly-hatched baby dinosaur not far from where we had built it. He said that it happened after he'd been digging deep in a sand bank to move some ground with the tractor, so he must have disturbed an area that hadn't been touched since the Ice Age. The dinosaur hadn't moved far from the remains of its egg and was the size of a small crocodile, but it didn't look like a lizard or a crocodile because it was smooth and brown and had a small head. It was alive, but still just looking around, so he was able to touch it.

I looked over at Dolores and to my astonishment, she was eagerly nodding in agreement. She piped up, "We were afraid it might bite if we tried to pick it up, so we left it there and went back up to the house to find something to put it in."

"And when you got back it was gone?" I asked the obvious question.

"It must have crawled off. I guess it could move quicker than I thought. Its tracks headed off in the direction of the Ute Mountain." Gene shook his head.

"And did you save any pieces of the egg?"

"No, we didn't think of that, did we Dolores."

"No, we didn't Gene."

And I had been worried about mountain lions and bears...

Gene farmed the land and taught John the ropes for at least a year after we moved into the house. I used to watch him move the water in the ditches to irrigate the fields from my kitchen window. It was a slow process, but he seemed to be out there to see what was going on as much as to get water to the alfalfa. Once, he sat down in the middle of a field in his yellow slicker to watch a big rainstorm, which came over the Ute Mountain. I kept an eye on him to make sure he got up when it was over.

We were both sad when they sold the trailer at the top and finally moved to town. Gene kept the ditches and fences in perfect order until the day he turned everything over to us. We rode horses with him one last time in the National Monument; and as we rounded the corner to come home, he said to us, "Look across the street, there's your farm."

7

I FOUND THE REMNANTS OF AN OLD ROAD in the southeast corner of the farm, which led towards the Ute Mountain. The red sand of the wide track, dotted with sage and cheet grass, stretched into the distance as far as I could see. I often walked there at dusk because I could imagine the ghosts of the Indian Nations receding up it to their teepees in the dark of the trees. I could hear them in certain parts of my farm at the right time of day.

Gene said that he remembered Navajo women silently filing past his trailer to camp on his land by the creek at the bottom. They would hunt a deer, cook it, share the meat with him, and sometimes stay for weeks at a time. Before the road was locked up in the dispute, some Ute boys would spend the night in a cave, which was hollowed out near the top of the stone face of the Battlerock. I could see them from my house, which had no curtains, and I still remember the tall shadows that they cast on the walls with the blazing fire in front.

One of my best friends, since the early days in Shiprock, was a beautiful woman who was half Navajo and half Ute. Her name was Janelle, and she had married the Irish grandson of a friend of my family, named Hal Doughty. Janelle and Hal moved into a proper house, from a primitive trailer without electricity, about the same time as we moved into ours. Amber and Lauren, their two oldest children, took me into their newly finished rooms so I could watch them turn on and off the lights.

I delivered three of Janelle's four children; her first daughter was born before we moved out West. When her first boy Lauren was born, she asked if I would call her brother Kevin and tell him that he had a son. Her English was perfect, so I thought perhaps the stress of labor had confused her. 'You mean a nephew', I reminded her. She was firm, 'No, I mean a son.' I found out later that the Navajo Way meant that all siblings were also mothers and fathers. I worried about eighteen year old Kevin even babysitting until I saw him taking care of Lauren one afternoon. He was tender, responsible, and infinitely patient with his 'son'.

They invited us to spend Christmas Eve with their family one year before we moved to Cortez. We brought a bottle of wine and a couple of crudely wrapped packages of plastic toys for the children. The trailer was cozy, if cramped, inside with a freshly cut pine tree covered in silver balls. We were handed a beautifully folded envelope and in it were papers for one of their horses; their Christmas present to us.

We were speechless, but Janelle wanted us to have him. She had raised him from a colt and loved him like an overgrown dog. His name was Handsome, and he became John's favorite horse of all time.

We moved him to the farm during the construction, and he walked around inside the houses before the doors were put up. Once, when we came to visit, he was looking at us from over the sink through the kitchen window; I was surprised he didn't try to go up the stairs. Until we had proper fencing on the road, he would race my truck to tear open the forty pound dog food bag in the back, then gorge himself on the spilled dry food on the road. He untied himself and the other horses any time we turned our backs on him; and when we moved in, he broke through any easy place in the fence around the houses so he could put his nose against our windows. He explored every inch of the farm and seemed eager to go out on the trails surrounding it.

The Battlerock was the most prominent part of our landscape, and it got its name after Navajo women and children threw themselves off the cliff and fell 600 feet to their death rather than be skinned and tortured by the Utes chasing them. There was a tree on the top shaped like a squaw holding a blanket over her arms in front of her. I could see it from my bedroom window, and it had been there as long as anyone could remember.

The Utes and the Navajo had battled for control of the area since their arrival in 1500. There was an armed peace between the few large-boned

Utes who lived on their mountain and the numerous lithe Navajo who lived on the desert land surrounding them, but no love lost between the two. We lived close to the border of both of their reservations.

The Navajo were incredibly hospitable when you were on their land. When we were in Shiprock, we cross-country skied in the Lukachukai Mountains in the winter and hiked in them during the summer. I remember once our dogs faced off with the dogs belonging to a Navajo shepherd with his flock. He took absolutely no notice and carried on talking to us about what a beautiful day it was.

The Utes were a different story. They arrested anyone they found trespassing in the best of circumstances and had been known to shoot and ask questions later in the worst.

That didn't stop me from crossing into Ute territory on a regular basis, but no one lived on the side of the Ute Mountain that faced our farm. I once asked Gene what I should do if I ever ran into a Ute on their side of the fence, and he told me to go to ground like a coyote and run down the nearest dry creek-bed.

" I couldn't just say I was looking for one of my dogs?"

"No, a man wouldn't want to chance running into a Ute up there by himself." He shook his head with concern.

This left me watching for human tracks even more closely than for those of a mountain lion, bear, or dinosaur; and fortunately, except for the dinosaur, they were much rarer.

8

JOHN GROANED WHEN THE ALARM CLOCK RANG AT FOUR.
"Why do we have to get up this early?"

"This isn't early to them, they get up with the chickens."

"Do you hear the chickens?"

"Maybe a little before the chickens, but they've been up all night with the Medicine Man. We would've had to stay all night too if we'd gone to see the cake mixed and put over the fire like you wanted to."

"I think we could've gone and left."

"Annie said that if we were there when the cake was made we had to stay until it was eaten. I didn't want to break their customs. What do we know about a Puberty Ceremony?"

That spring in 1994 was much dryer than the year before, but still cold in the mornings in May. We pulled on jeans and sweaters and figured there'd be plenty of coffee at Annie's house. The directions were as vague as usual. We were supposed to go to Shiprock, turn at East Low Rent Housing, follow the road for a mile or two then head south on a dirt road marked with an upright tire. Her driveway was the first one on the right, and miraculously, we found it in the dark. Three dogs bounded over when we drove in the yard.

There were a couple of guys standing around outside, and the lights shone from both rooms of the box-shaped house. The men said nothing to us as we passed them, and the house was full of women I didn't know. One of them went to find Annie.

The Navajo plan their Puberty Ceremony soon after a girl gets her first period. Annie was one of my favorite nurses in Shiprock, and she had two daughters. She asked me to come to the ceremony when the first one came of age, and I eagerly accepted.

When the Navajo were successfully rebuilding their population to upwards of two hundred and ten thousand, from only seven thousand after their internment at Bosco Redondo, encouraging pregnancy as soon as possible was part of the plan. The Puberty Ceremony emphasized to young women their significance as carriers of the culture and their responsibility to ensure the survival of the Navajo people. Annie described the actual ceremony to me a few days before in the clinic.

"The Medicine Man comes in the evening, and the men start the fire for the cake. The women mix up the cake, and the Medicine Man blesses it and spreads it over the fire."

"What's the cake made of?" I had been informed by Anglos that it was inedible.

"It's made of ground corn, flour, wheat kernels, and honey."

"And it cooks all night?"

"Yes, the ceremony starts when the cake is made and goes on all night long. We don't eat it until the morning. First, my daughter lies down on a blanket, and the Medicine Man stretches her. Then she runs across the desert towards the sun..."

"The Medicine Man stretches her?" My eyes widened. I was, after all, a Gynecologist and had been told this was in preparation for becoming sexually active and pregnant.

"To make her tall." I thanked God that Annie hadn't noticed the indignation in my voice. I told her we would come in the morning, watch the last part, and eat the cake.

There was no conversation in the front room as we waited for Annie to appear. John felt uncomfortable and went to stand outside. I sat and reminded myself that the Navajo people had no problem with absolute silence.

Annie looked tired when she came in from the round adobe Hogan across the yard where the ceremony was being held. She ran to the back room, returned with a beautifully woven Navajo wedding basket, and handed it to me. I looked at her quizzically, and she explained that I needed to remove my jewelry. I slipped off my watch and put it inside.

We went outside to stand around the fire for warmth in the half-light of the dawn. It gave off limited heat because the top was entirely covered by a thick layer of cake whose margins were indistinct from the surrounding sand. Annie's daughter emerged from the Hogan, and the Medicine Man brushed her hair and chanted a high-pitched Navajo blessing before she ran across the desert.

The men started tearing up cardboard boxes, and I wondered what was happening next. They picked up some shovels that were leaning against the house and started cutting the cake into brick-sized segments. John called me from across the fire to stand by his side. The slabs of 'cake' were put on the torn boxes and handed out around the circle. John seemed particularly concerned about the piece we got, and it felt heavy and bland in my mouth when I tasted it.

We stayed for another half hour, pretended to eat some more, then told them we needed to get back. Annie wrapped the cake up, so we could take it home for later. I was too shy to ask for my watch back and wondered if it was meant to be a gift, so I left it behind. We waved good-bye to everyone standing quietly in the sandy yard that was now the color of deer-hide with the rising sun. The truck was immediately filled with noise as we eagerly discussed breakfast at the diner down the road.

"Why were you so concerned about the piece we got? They all looked the same size to me." I thought that John was trying for the smallest one.

"When I was standing by the fire on my own, the cat came and pissed on the other side of the cake."

We had to pull over we were laughing so hard.

The chickens thought the cake was delicious, and Annie returned my watch to me on Monday. A few months later, her second daughter had a Puberty Ceremony and I told her I was sorry that I had to miss it. She was beaming in the clinic the Monday after the second ceremony. She produced a torn box with a heavy slab covered in foil and said she had saved me some cake.

9

I WAS STILL WORKING on the Navajo Reservation when we moved to the farm. Our property was fifty miles north of Shiprock, so my commute to the Navajo hospital was almost an hour in either direction. I was on-call every fourth night and every fourth weekend, which meant countless nights in a one room apartment that resembled a monk's cell on the Reservation. The monthly weekends began to seem endless, and I became exhausted from all the driving.

Our farm was also eighteen miles west of Cortez, a border town in Colorado. After a year, the local hospital in Cortez got wind of an Obstetrician/Gynecologist close-by. They approached me, and I agreed to open a practice.

Medicine was my anchor, my credibility, my barometer on the lives of others, my security, and my big book with a thousand unfolding stories. In spite of its unexpected twists and inevitable disappointments, I loved Medicine unconditionally; it was the essence of my life.

My father was a self-made man who respected no law or custom. He was so adamant about there being no God that he had us call him 'God' instead. My mother was a Southern intellectual who had been steeped in snobbery and valued decorum. Once, she overheard me cursing and wept to think she'd raised a daughter with a 'trash mouth'. Neither of them was particularly excited about my choice to go to medical school.

I had seizures as a child and thought that I would never drive a car, much less be a doctor. When they miraculously disappeared at age eighteen, I felt so fortunate that I never looked back.

Getting a residency at Cornell in New York City was called 'shooting the moon', especially for a Southerner, because of the competition. When

I found out that I was accepted on the day of the Resident Match in April of my last year of medical school, I screamed and ran out of the auditorium crying with happiness.

I'll always remember my first hysterectomy during the residency training. I had recently read an article postulating that the 'fight or flight' response was interpreted differently by girls and boys because of early conditioning. The boys, when asked "Aren't you excited!" in challenging situations, interpreted the dry mouth, sweating, and racing heart as excitement. The girls, in similar circumstances, were more often asked, "Aren't you afraid?" I was determined to be 'excited' with my racing pulse and sweaty palms .

In addition, the physicians who were in charge of my training in New York imposed the psychological trauma that should have happened in Kindergarten; they switched me from being left-handed to being right-handed. They assured me that the last thing I wanted to be known as was a 'left-handed surgeon'. I began using my right hand to experiment with suture, forceps, and needle drivers on bits of cloth in all my spare time. Sutured cloth and knotted thread littered everywhere I lingered.

That first surgical patient in New York spoke only a little English with a heavy Spanish accent. She had fibroids, bleeding, and anemia. I walked into her cubicle looking studiously at her chart.

"Looks like you've been bleeding a lot."

"Yes, it's terrible." Or did she say 'horrible'? It was difficult to tell.

"Your ultrasound shows fibroids or muscle overgrowths in your uterus, making it the size of a grapefruit instead of a lime. The heavy bleeding is from the fibroids, and most of the time the only way to stop the bleeding is to do a hysterectomy; remove your uterus with the fibroids growing inside it."

"Whatever you think, Doctor." I wondered if she had understood. Were the fruit names the same in Spanish?

"Well, I do think we need to operate to make things better."

"Who operay?" She looked at me incredulously.

"Me?" I tried not to make it sound like a question, but it did anyway. I also inadvertently glanced over my shoulder hoping to find someone more convincing behind me.

Miraculously, at the end of four years, I felt comfortable and competent. I finished my residency at New York Hospital with gratitude to all who had helped along the way and a strong belief in the right to national health care. This was ironic as it was the one of the most prestigious private hospitals in the city. I had been honored to be one of the six interns chosen from hundreds of applicants across the country and had thoroughly enjoyed the training; it was the uneven delivery of medical care that I rejected. In 1988, when I left to practice with the National Health Service in England, I was convinced that I would never come back. We sold all our worldly goods and travelled across the Atlantic with only a few talismans.

My job in Somerset was an hour commute from a place that John and I both loved on the north Devon coast. We rented a cottage that had been a Methodist church in a previous life, complete with a lectern. The thatched village was full of flowers and had fields that led down to the sea.

I worked as a Registrar, which was little difference from the Chief Resident year I had just completed, but I was eager to learn the ropes of the English system. I was disappointed after only a few short months to find that the sheer volume of patients and the paucity of doctors made giving good care practically impossible. There weren't enough hours in the day and night combined.

While we were there, we bought a Labrador Retriever puppy who was like our first child. When John wasn't writing, he was out on the hills with Sam who was a quiet, intelligent soul and very good company. After a year in England, we both decided that it wasn't the life we had envisioned. We made plans to leave and return to America over the next few months. Of course, Sam came with us.

In July of 1990, when we moved from England to New Mexico, we flew to the South then drove across country. Sam was in shock from the heat. Our car had no air conditioning, so we stopped at gas stations every two hours to douse him down with hoses. Our house had no air conditioning either, so he spent most of his time the first few months drinking water and panting.

The house was made of cement block and had a picture window, which looked out on the Shiprock to the west and let in the burning heat of the long afternoons. It sat on a compound close to the hospital, we had a backyard surrounded by chain-link fence, and the furniture was from the local women's shelter. John was fascinated by the Reservation. He took a course to learn Navajo, made lots of friends, and hunted ducks with Sam when he wasn't working on his novel. I embraced the simplicity and celebrated having fewer keys.

A clause in a treaty with the Native Americans promised to protect their health and well-being. This evolved into the Indian Health Service, which gave anyone enrolled in a tribe healthcare free of charge. The hospital and clinics in Shiprock were a collection of cheap buildings and trailers that looked like a M.A.S.H. unit. I walked to work there each morning among stray dogs and errant sprinklers.

During one of my first medical staff meetings, we were encouraged to sign our patients up for Medicaid. Because most Native Americans were below the poverty level and very few owned land or houses, almost all of them qualified. The Medical Director drew different sized boxes on a flip chart to illustrate how our inadequate funding was resolved by double dipping.

Over my five years there I discovered that although we gave good care in Shiprock, it cost too much to do it. And it continued to bother me that we made up the deficit by taking from one Government pocket to feed another.

When I made the decision to work in Cortez, I had serious doubts about joining the system that I had rejected, but nothing I had seen had worked so far. I rationalized that it might deepen my understanding of mainstream healthcare and hoped that I could still be viable commercially and see the under-served. I bought a house downtown to turn into an office, hired staff, and hung out a shingle like in the days of old. I started seeing patients in February of 1995.

The first C-section I did there was also a memorable experience. It was in the middle of the night, so there wasn't much chatter in the Operating

Room. I easily finished in twenty minutes and said, "We're done."

"You're done?" The O.R. crew exclaimed in unison.

"I think I'm done. Is there anything else you'd like me to do?"

"It usually takes at least an hour for a C-section; sometimes two." Their eyes smiled over the top of the masks; they couldn't believe their luck.

I was the first Ob/Gyn to come to Cortez and the only one for fifty miles. The General Surgeons and Family Practitioners had done the C-sections there for years, but it took a lot longer. Because it was such an ego boost to be congratulated for garden-variety skills in Obstetrics, I couldn't wait to show them what else I could do.

And over the next five years, I certainly did. I decided to do solo Obstetrics and take on the responsibility of almost all the C-sections in the community. It worked financially because we needed the money to pay off the farm and worked professionally to develop a patient base. I gave up everything for twenty-four hours a day, seven days a week. The farm was twenty-five minutes from the hospital and I needed to get there in thirty minutes for the C-sections, so I couldn't even walk to the edge of my property. There was no hiking, no riding, no drinking, no travel, and very little sleep.

10

MY OFFICE WAS IN AN OLD HOUSE; the entrance flanked by climbing yellow roses and honeysuckle. I wrote my notes in a green tiled kitchen and moved quietly across the waxed wooden floors. I could usually tell when a patient arrived by the slap of the screen door in the front. I felt happy to get there every morning and enjoyed the pace I set throughout the day.

When I first started, I had so few patients it terrified me. The mortgage on the office, plus the equipment and supplies, added to my already unmanageable debt; and I had no idea how to run a business and no money for an office manager. I hired a secretary and nurse, started studying medical coding and payroll, and enrolled in courses on insurance and reimbursement.

My 1930s stucco house was on an established block behind Main Street in downtown Cortez, one of the poorest towns in Colorado. The road from Shiprock to Durango ran straight through it and became Main for about four stoplights. There were two hunting stores facing each other on either side of the street, a Chinese restaurant, and a couple of western cafes. The Tomahawk Inn and a few trading posts, where the Navajo and Ute sold their wares, were further down the road towards Shiprock; and Walmart and Wendy's towards Durango. The billboards on the way into town from both directions boasted of it being at the foot of Mesa Verde and right next to the Ute and Navajo Reservations, but location notwithstanding, it remained undiscovered.

I took all comers which meant I had many Medicaid and Medicare patients and quite a number of uninsured. Joann, my secretary, patiently worked out no-interest payment plans for my patients that could potentially span twenty years; and Kierra, my nurse, knew everyone in town and their sad stories. I learned that some of the poorest patients were the most reliable to pay. I received monthly hundred dollar checks from laborers until thousand dollar bills were resolved, and there was a sense of honor among the ranchers who were land-rich, but cash-poor.

John and I used to open Friday's mail at a picnic table in the Cortez Park on Saturday mornings and total up the cash receipts for the week. We laughed at the precariousness of our situation and embraced the 'No Fear' attitude recommended by bumper stickers on the cars which were kitted out for extreme sports and heading towards Durango.

My patients turned out to be a mix of ranchers, city-dwellers who had moved to Telluride, and Native Americans. I saw very few people from Durango as it had its own Ob/Gyn practice.

The country women exchanged stories with me about the things that followed the seasons. In the late summer, I got tips on bottling tomatoes and putting up fruit. In the fall, we discussed riding trails, hunting seasons, and recipes for jerky. The amount of snowfall high in the mountains and reservoir fill were the topics of the winter. And the spring brought tales of burning irrigation ditches, sand storms, and setting onions and potatoes.

The New-Age Telluride group kept me amused by playing chimes during the pap smears and feeling superior because they menstruated with the full moon. One or two of them even drank their own first morning urine to detoxify themselves.

My Native American patients in Cortez were almost all from the Mountain Ute tribe. Most of the Navajo went to the hospital in Shiprock, which wasn't too far away. The Utes could have gone there as well, but they complained of ill treatment from the Navajo nurses and had Medicaid, so they preferred to use the Cortez hospital instead. It was also a little bit closer.

I found the Utes more inscrutable than the Navajo, which was saying a lot. I remember the movie 'The Missing' making an impression on me one night after we moved to the farm. The Apache villain and authentic New Mexico landscape made me imagine a rogue Ute was going to descend from his mountain across the creek and roast us in burlap sacks. Afterwards, I was called to a C-section at around two in the morning and nervously walked to the car in the dark. I got to the hospital, changed into scrubs, and went to stare at the TV and wait for the Anesthetist and the nurses to get everything ready. The Ute father of the baby appeared from the men's changing room, and I recognized him from the Sun Dance a few months before.

We were included in a handful of Anglos who had been invited to the top of the Ute Mountain to watch the men who went without food or water for four days. They first had a dream of their Sun Dance then were accepted to do the ceremony. It was held by a mountain lake deep in Ute territory. Young braves held their throats and gave battle calls to freak us out as we drove past them walking there.

We were led into a tent made of bleached canvas stretched over freshly cut, arched aspen branches with dangling, heart-shaped leaves. There was a huge fire inside; and, at first, I was afraid of the noise of the drums and the wild chanting. The Ute warriors moved back and forth in a trance to challenge a beautifully painted pole in the center, then they rested on their blankets surrounding it. I was as hypnotized as they were in the end and found it hard to leave.

I felt certain he had been one of the dancers, but he looked so different in purple scrubs. I remained silent and eyed him with newfound suspicion. He sat down quietly next to me. I looked again and saw a vulnerable twenty year old who hadn't slept in two nights. I smiled and made a joke about the TV program. He beamed, "Are you the doctor? You're going to do the C-section? We've been waiting for two days for this baby. We're naming him 'Wambly.' It's the Ute word for eagle."

11

THERE WERE MORE ANIMALS THAN PEOPLE in our neck of the woods; and we did our part by bringing five dogs, three horses, two cats, and eight chickens when we came. Sam had watched with resignation as we adopted a new puppy every year in Shiprock. The first year, I found Beth, a German shepherd mix, begging for food outside the hospital. She was so skinny that she was all ears, and it had been so long since she'd eaten that she couldn't keep anything down for the first two days.

The second year, Dusty, an English shepherd mix, was dropped inside the chain link fence in our backyard. She was an unweaned ball of black and white fluff who was too young to even whimper. Beth ruled her with an iron fist, but seemed happy to stand in, save nursing, as her mother.

Years three and four brought Jessie and Max. Jessie, a Labrador mix, was a small black chewing machine, with the speed and fury of the Tasmanian devil, who appeared on the doorstep. And Max, a Brittany, quivered with nervous energy when we scooped him up into the truck. All five dogs must have thought they'd arrived in heaven when we moved them to the farm. Sam still acted as if it was occasionally too hot for his English blood.

By the time we made the move, we also had three horses. Handsome was such an adorable horse that we immediately searched for a Navajo pony for me. When we were first looking at horses at the sale barns close-by, they were bidding on most of them for meat. I left quite a few crying over colts with broken legs.

We found my horse, Sage, in a town called Egnar which was 'Range' spelled backwards. An old cowboy sold us both her and her daughter because they'd never been parted. Before he'd had her and bred her, she belonged to a Navajo grandmother or 'shama' as the older women are called.

She was a beautiful buckskin mare whose sweet brown eyes had such perfect dark shadows around them that she looked like she was wearing eye make-up. Her daughter was a larger, multi-colored horse that we called 'Paint' for obvious reasons. Handsome ran the mares around the farm to show his dominance for about a week after their arrival; but, true to their gender, they quickly learned how to get around him.

We had adopted just two cats out of a multitude that passed through our yard on the reservation. They were a matching grey color and could have been father and daughter. They meowed loudly from their cardboard boxes on the back seat of the car in the move from Shiprock. We put them next to the ones with the chickens inside which had only the occasional thump.

In a short time, our charges had settled down nicely. We put the dogs in kennels at night, the cats spent most of their time indoors, and our assorted chickens stayed close to the house. But the eighty acres seemed to be begging for more use, so John quickly became more interested in raising animals than writing.

He thought that there must be many undiscovered great Navajo horses like Handsome and Sage, so he decided to scour the Reservation in search of more ponies. The idea was to buy them cheap, smooth out any rough edges, then sell them on to Anglo newcomers for trail riding. I was eager to learn about each and every horse, so the plan sounded good to me. Through Gene, we heard of a shady horse trader named Tony. In the past he was rumored to have stolen horses by the trailer-full that he disguised by spray-painting them a different color, but Gene said he had changed his ways.

We drove twelve miles west from the house to the Utah portion of the Navajo Reservation. Ismay Trading Post was on the dividing line in the dust with its twin piles of broken glass on either side of the door. After a lonely crossroads in Montezuma Creek, we found a painted white tire lying in the sand that marked Tony's driveway. It ascended a stony mesa and seemed to go on for miles. I began to wonder if Tony might exist only in Gene's imagination.

We finally got to a collection of randomly placed trailers, campers, and corrals. A gnome-like Navajo cowboy in a big hat appeared in the open doorway of one of them. He didn't speak much English and kept calling John my 'boss.' His horses were small and rank. They bucked from the time John got on them until he bailed off in the bushes. Although Tony's horses were as cheap as Gene said, they weren't even worth the price he was asking.

Eventually, between the Cortez Sale Barn and more productive Navajo sources, we had a few horses to work with. We built corrals and put up fences, but half of the horses had intractable bad habits and the other half were injury prone. I spent hours in the field trying to befriend them and weeks cleaning out fist-sized wounds with wire wool. The horse business was much rougher than I imagined, and John eventually lost interest too.

We more often ate the eggs than our chickens, so our next plan was to raise rabbits for food. We built adjoining, spacious, wooden hutches on silts and bought two lop-eared ones from the farm store; a male and a female to start. The dogs were all interested, but Max and Beth were the hardest to distract. Max was a spaniel and an avid hunter. He stayed under the cage without moving for the first three days after they arrived.

Beth must have been a German Shepherd mixed with a coyote because there was nothing she liked better than chasing rabbits. You would see her jumping vertically with her front paws poised to pounce then hear her terrifying, shrill yipping when she was in full pursuit. She caught many in her time, and they quickly disappeared down her throat. She chewed them up eating everything in order; fur, bones, limbs, and head;. The last thing you saw was the ears bobbing their way into her mouth.

Our rabbits had several litters, and we ate a few, but it was hard to keep them healthy. They had a tendency towards abscesses and respiratory illness, and their numbers dwindled. John butchered the last one right before he left on a trip. He gutted it, left it in the refrigerator, and explained to me how to skin it.

I had watched him do it, but felt unsure about how to proceed. I lined up my instruments simulating a surgical procedure. I used the cleaver to chop off the legs and slipped the cold skin off with my fingers. As I worked, I talked myself through all of the steps. The little bit of gut that John left near the rectum was removed with true surgical precision. After I finished, I threw all the leftover bits to the dogs. We felt silly not giving them bones after watching whole animals disappear down their throats.

The rabbit hutches were broken up for firewood; and before I knew it, John bought Watusi cattle from a friend because he'd always wanted to run cows. At that point, I was pretty disenchanted by the amount of work involved in keeping animals and the fact that, so far, they had only cost money and not brought any in.

"Mark says these cows are sure winners. You use the body for meat and still have the skull with huge horns to sell for a fortune in Santa Fe."

"So we're going to have rotting heads hanging all over the farm? I knew now to anticipate the nitty-gritty.

"We've got plenty of space. What about down by the creek at the bottom?"

"I pass by there all the time when I go hiking. I could give them a pat and remember what nice cows they were."

"I'm not sure they're such nice cows."

Six of them arrived, crowded together in a horse trailer. When they got off, they ran into the field straight towards where we were standing. We were all terrified and scrambled across the fence.

They were mean, and they looked deadly. There was no way to be around them on foot, so we had to move them from one pasture to another on horseback. We reinforced the fences, built corrals around easily climbable trees, and put in special cattle chutes; big gates which pressed together to hold them still so you could doctor them without risking life and limb.

I remember coming home one afternoon to the news that the cows were out again.

"Well John, you've been here all day."

"But Sage is so good with them. You might not even need a saddle."

"How far away are they?"

"Oh, a couple miles up the road, but they'll be easy to gather."

"I'm from the South. I didn't watch much Bonanza as a child. And I'm on call."

"I don't think it'll take long. You like to ride."

"On trails, not moving cows. What if I get called from the hospital?" Which I inevitably did.

"Emily, we have a patient of yours in labor. She's early yet." The labor room nurse sounded reassuring.

"That's a relief."

"Why is your voice shaking?"

"I'm moving cows. Down the road. On a horse. I need to go before I drop the cellphone. I'll call you back as soon as I can."

The cows turned out to be another financial disaster. We managed to sell them and their calves to the local rodeo, but the round-up fences and cattle chute sat unused as painful reminders. We were probably lucky to come out of it in one piece.

12

SOON AFTER WE MOVED TO THE FARM, our Navajo 'son' appeared. His name was Winson, and he showed up with his father one day and asked if we needed some help. He was a tall skinny nineteen year old who looked younger than his years; he could have just stepped off a junior high athletic field. His handsome face had high cheekbones which were accentuated by his closely cropped hair. For some reason, David, the father, had changed the family's last name to Filfred, then named the sons: Winsonfred, Winfred, Wilfred, Gilfred, and Philfred. Winson, short for Winsonfred, started work that day; and before we all knew it, it had stretched into years.

He worked hard and enjoyed stretching fence and baling hay. He was soft-spoken, laughed easily, and never got frustrated. The dogs and horses loved him and soon he was part of the family. The three of us rode horses together on Ute Mountain, and he often stayed over for dinner. He tried my French and Mexican dishes and challenged me to hot chile-eating contests. John called him 'son' and was always giving him advice.

On the weekends, he would bring his younger brother Winfred to work with him. I could hear them during the day from the house. They kidded around in Navajo and laughed a lot. They also sang Navajo songs, sometimes low and calm, sometimes at the top of their lungs.

Navajo culture was of utmost importance to Winson. He spent countless hours telling us about Native American religion and the four spirits of the earth. He tried to explain what happened at an all-night squaw dance and the rules for the Navajo shoe game. In the middle of a riveting description of a three day salt trail on horseback, he would break the spell by mixing centuries; "And when we finally rode back into the camp, they threw our reward onto the sand in front of us. We were so happy because it was lots of boxes of Crackerjacks."

Before long, through Winson and Winfred, John knew all the Filfreds and their cousins. He immersed himself in their world for a while and spent time in Aneth and Montezuma Creek; the Navajo towns fifteen miles down the road after the Utah border. He watched them hunt for deer and rabbit and learned how they butchered sheep and cattle. He rode with them on desert trails and helped them doctor their horses.

After his first sweat lodge with them, he was eager to tell me the story when I got home from work.

"You know how with traditional sweat lodges everyone is naked."

"Yeah, that's why they don't mix the men and the women. And also why I've never been to one."

"Well, when I undressed, they shrieked and covered their eyes when they saw my circumcision."

"I can't say I remember doing any circumcisions on the Navajo when I was in Shiprock. It must've looked pretty strange to them."

"They made me wind it round and round with wool before they'd let me go inside." John was laughing.

"That must have been funny looking."

"I think it was. Maybe they were just having me on, but they seemed truly disgusted. The wool came off when we rolled in the sand afterwards, and they made me put it back on again."

"Did you wear it home?" Unfortunately, he shook his head no.

John was genuinely interested in everything. He could remember history so accurately that he could match the dates to the year in the 'Timetables of History' book that we had upstairs. He knew every piece of significant literature and devoured tomes of history and politics. He was also wealth of information on old movies, ballet, music, and plays. He could amuse any cab driver in any country with some knowledge of their customs; be it sports, food, or current events. And he was most at home outdoors; he knew every type of grass, flower, bird, and animal. He could see deer like the Navajo when they were only spots on the hillside.

We were both proud, but sad, when Winson told us that he had decided to train to be a policemen so he could help his people. We missed him when he was doing his training in New Mexico, but were happy when he dropped by to show us his muscles and boast of the rigorousness of the program. Winfred filled in for us when he could, but he was a football star at his high school in Aneth, so he didn't have much spare time.

After he finished at the Police Academy, Winson got married and had a child in less than a year. He brought his new wife and son to the farm to meet us soon after the baby was born. His wife was shy and had buck teeth and glasses. His son looked exactly like him and also seemed to have the same good nature. We didn't see as much of him after he started work as a policeman in Kayenta. Between his new family and work, he was incredibly busy.

Then one day, David, his father, came with Winson's mother; and they got out of the truck and leaned on it for support. They told us the story of how Winson was called to two fires in one day. The second time, he was totally exhausted. He was driving through thick fog on the road to Kayenta and didn't see an RV that was parked just off the highway until it was too late. He died instantly in the crash.

His parents made the trip, only a day after he died, because they knew we were like a second set of parents to him. I was too emotional to attend the funeral. John said the people stretched for miles down the road, but he had a special seat in front with the family. His father and brothers rode up to the grave, chanting in Navajo, with his riderless horse; and the whole police force was there with a military band to play Taps.

I had an old, red Toyota pick-up that I loved, and I gave it to Winfred much like Janelle gave us the horse. Winfred was never the same after Winson died. He worked for us for a few more months, then I only saw him when my red pick-up was coming down the canyon road.

I often imagined Winson with me when I walked on the farm in the evenings. There was a ghost in the guest-house tower after he died; no one slept well because of the noise. An artist from Santa Fe had painted a large portrait of Winson, which hung on the second floor, so I was sure the ghost was him. He liked playing basketball, and in the mornings my guests would invariably describe the sound of a bouncing ball.

13

WE PLANTED SOME FRUIT TREES around the house the first year, and they thrived in a surprisingly short period of time. We decided to put in a proper orchard and large kitchen garden to see what else worked out West. We tried an interesting combination of English and Southern fruits and vegetables over the years; black currants, gooseberries, broad beans, okra, yellow squash, and white peaches. Some of the English choices seemed to call out to me for shade and water every time I passed them by.

McElmo Canyon had produced much of the food for Cortez over the years, but everything needed water. We bucketed the trees and garden for the first few years, then put in a drip line and sprinkler system when we switched the hay fields to side roll irrigation. We had the oldest ditch rights in the Montezuma County, which is what Gene meant when he said the farm was on the number one ditch. The irrigation water and McElmo creek created a green strip of oasis between the Ute Mountain range on one side and the red canyons of the Monument on the other.

Our idea of a great weekend in the fall was to gather up all the horse and chicken manure from around the farm and spread it on the beds for the next year. We continued to refine what we planted according to our great success with some things and failure with others. It was soon evident that the amount of work involved in no way matched the potential return. We would proudly pile our home-grown produce on the kitchen table and occasionally even photograph it, but we were hardly going to sit for hours with four zucchini at the Cortez farmer's market.

Like all farmers, we continued to grow and enjoy our own bounty, but it was for love not money. In the spring, I filled the house with vases of branches pruned from the fruit trees in order to watch them blossom. I harvested and sewed pungent lavender into small bags for my drawers, so it would remind me of summer each time I opened them. And I plunged colorful jars of fruits and vegetables into water baths in the fall, so we could still eat our own food in the winter.

A large portion of what we ate came from the land, not the grocery store. In addition to our eggs and what we grew, there were many things in the wild that we took advantage of. The original settlers had brought asparagus and watercress, which still thrived along the banks of the ditch and in nooks of barely rippling water. There were scores of edible mushrooms; shaggy inkcaps, puffballs, chanterelles, and cepes. I picked bagfuls of lamb's ear greens in the spring, which we ate cooked and raw in salads. Trout were a staple except in the dead of winter. And most of our meat came from hunting.

The adjoining property to our eastern side belonged to an old ranching family and was one of many parcels the family had down the canyon. The creek had formed ponds at the bottom which they dammed for the cattle. The first time John strayed over there, he came back beaming.

"I took the dogs over to that low place of Wesley's, and it's like St. James's Park in London!"

"How could it be like St. James's Park? You've lost your marbles."

"There is every variety of duck just paddling around in circles. I've got to go back there and hunt tomorrow."

"You'd better clear it with Wesley first."

"I'm sure he won't mind. He's a lot easier to deal with than Betty."

John asked him about hunting, and he said we could do whatever we liked as long as we didn't shoot his cows. It became a Thanksgiving tradition to buy all the trimmings, but no bird. We would go out early in the morning with Sam and wait for the ducks to come in.

I never shot, but was happy to be along whispering with John behind the reeds, listening for the ducks calling in the distance, being fully aware of the dawn, and snuggling up to Sam who was incredible to watch when he was working. If we got no ducks, there were only vegetables for dinner, but we rarely came home empty-handed.

The meat from one deer or an elk would get the two of us through the winter. John hunted for those with the Navajo and brought them back field-dressed. We would hang the carcass in the cool air outside for a couple of days, just high enough so the dogs wouldn't tear at it but could still chase away the magpies. Butchering, parceling, and labeling everything was an all day affair; but I always felt a sense of security and accomplishment when it was neatly stacked in the freezer.

Death was part of our daily existence. I saw Gene's lambs playing at the barn in the morning only to be butchered in the afternoon. I looked with awe at the beautiful blue feathers on the warm teal that Sam carefully put into my outstretched hand. I witnessed the same process in nature. I passed by piles of feathers, clumps of dried skin and fur, I saw the dark stain of blood on the ground at the edge of a field where a lion jumped an unsuspecting deer.

I felt schizophrenic when trying to save injured baby birds and rabbits or owls with broken wings; but I yearned for nothing to suffer, die, or change even if I knew it wasn't possible. I wanted my green felt farm from childhood with stick-on happy animals and people that were always the same. I loved everything so much it scared me.

One beautiful season followed another, and I studied them intensely marking the familiar pattern and the unique variation of each year. I watched the land with rapt attention, knew the paths the animals took, understood their cycles and habits; heard the coyote pups in the spring, saw the fawn's footprints alongside the mother, watched for fresh teeth marks in the trees by the creek as the beavers made their dams. When I was on the hill with the dogs, I felt I had bridged the gap and was one of them. We looked at the tufts of hair left behind by a passing deer, sniffed the air for fresh scent, and sat on hillsides in bunches watching.

I kept asking myself: Was it possible to love things too much? Was it possible to be too happy? My life was uncannily perfect, but the uncanny part made me certain it couldn't last exactly as it was. I was never unaware of the fact that Fate was treating me kindly, and everything could be different tomorrow. Was that all the more reason to embrace it, or not to trust it? I decided to embrace it and not take a single moment for granted.

I put my faith in learning everything I could about this new life that I was able to experience with such intensity. I reveled in hearing, seeing, smelling, touching, and tasting. I had never felt more alive, and it was the most attached I'd been to a person, a place, and a way of living. I made the decision that fear in the face of all the goodness bestowed upon me seemed ungrateful.

I remember at the time I was reading a book by Arthur Koestler called 'The Lotus and the Robot' and trying to digest the Hindu concept of detachment. It seemed more foreign to me than ever. I didn't want to cut myself off from everything in life to simulate death. I had the rest of time to be dead.

14

IN THE BEGINNING OF JUNE IN 1995, we had lived on the farm for two years. My practice was bringing a little income, and John had a good grasp of what was required to farm the land. Our house still didn't have much furniture and was decorated with oats and rye that we had picked from the fields and dried. We left all the fans running in the house at night to try to battle the heat.

One Saturday morning, I slipped quietly out of bed and tiptoed to the kitchen and put on the tea. I had baked bread the night before. I cut thick slices, toasted them, and put them on a tray with the jam from last year's apricots. John's birthday present, a Leatherman knife, was small enough to fit in one corner. I brought the tray into him; the china clinking in time with my footsteps. Since as early as age ten, with my parents, I had always loved bringing people breakfast in bed.

I was overjoyed that I didn't have to leave the farm all day. I had no post-operative patients in the hospital and none of my obstetrical patients were due. I had done all my grocery shopping with carefully constructed lists on Friday after work. After breakfast, we went out to feed the horses and chickens and let the dogs out of their cages. All the animals seemed overjoyed too. The mornings in early June were sublime.

John needed to do some work on the fences close to the house. I went back inside to start the preparations for his birthday dinner. I put on Puccini's opera 'La Boheme' at a comfortable volume and started assembling my ingredients. John stopped by the kitchen on his way to irrigate the top fields and asked what I was making. Without giving away too many details, I told him it was the Mexican sauce, mole.

It was still cool in the kitchen. I studied the cookbook carefully and tried to work my way through the sequence of steps in the three page recipe. I put all the ingredients out on the butcher block table in the middle of the kitchen and arranged them in their order of appearance. I made slow progress roasting then soaking three different types of chiles, passing them through a sieve, roasting and grinding the nuts, melting the chocolate, and crushing the spices with a mortar and pestle. The first half of the opera finished and I clicked in the second CD.

John returned around noon with the morning irrigation completed and asked, "What are you making now?"

"The same mole." At least it would be enough for more than one meal.

We sat in the shade on the porch for lunch with the dogs under our feet. The Ute Mountain rose up in front of us, and the creek shone in the sun at the bottom. The table was strewn with bread, cheese, salami, the first spring arugula, and piles of asparagus from the banks of the irrigation ditches.

After lunch, John went out to get water to the fields at the bottom and I resumed making the mole. I only had a few steps left. I then cooked and pulled the chicken and made quick work of preparing the flan since it was old hat. I went out and gathered a huge bunch of wild sunflowers and put them in an oversized vase on the dining room table. John finished his work for the day; and we were both feeling sleepy, so we lay on the sofas across from each other in the coolest part of the house, read for a few minutes, then napped.

I fed the dogs around six, and John had a beer on the porch. I showered again because I smelled of roasted chiles and put on a black dress for dinner.

"Where'd you get that dress?"

"It's from the thrift shop in Telluride."

"Very French housewife."

"I know. I thought about pearls, but didn't want to be overdressed."

We had a lovely dinner, just the two of us, at one end of the table with the various dishes at the other end within arm's reach. We let all the dogs in the house before putting them up for the night. They must have wondered about the occasion.

The creek sounded loud from the porch as we sipped brandy and ate flan in the light of the half moon.

"You were running restaurants in Charleston and New York, and now you're irrigating fields."

"You were at a prestigious hospital in New York for four years. We could always go back to that life if we wanted to, but it's not what we've chosen."

"Are you happy?"

"Of course. You know a life farming has always been my dream. Are you?"

"Happier than I could ever have imagined."

15

THE VINEYARD BEGAN IN 1996 as a decorative idea for the ground around the houses that sloped down to the creek. We spoke to a friend in Napa and the experts in Grand Junction; and it turned into a grand plan before we knew it. Each vine needed its own water source, so ponds were dug, underground irrigation lines were placed, and drip lines were strung. The ground needed to be prepared, endless posts had to be sunk, high tensile wire stretched, and holes dug. We had to decide on how many vines to plant, what varietals might do best, on grafted versus non-grafted stock; even deciding how much water to give them through the drip system was a shot in the dark.

No one had planted vines in the Four Corners before. It was far-fetched for many reasons, not the least of which was the altitude of 5,500 feet. And another far-fetched plan was not what I wanted, but I was swept away by John's enthusiasm as I had been so many times before during our years together. My practice was our sole support, and I was taking care of a community where the main sources of employment were the hospital, Walmart and the grocery store. A vineyard added countless years to my struggle to keep up with the debt.

We planted a thousand vines, mostly Merlot with a couple of rows of Cabernet Franc. We picked enough grapes in 1997 to fill a large green trashcan and pushed the skins down into the juice three times a day with a garden rake. I found a handwritten note, posted at our local grocery store, advertising an apple press for sale. When we pressed our fermented grapes through it, as much got on the floor as in the container.

John held a wine glass under the spout to collect some of the stream, tasted it, and said, "You're not going to believe this."

He handed me the glass. The red liquid looked cloudy and had some debris in the bottom, so I feared the worst. I took a small sip, and it seemed okay so I took a big mouthful. "It's okay!"

I handed the glass back to him. He swirled it around and drank it again and said, "It's better than okay. You wouldn't send it back in a restaurant!"

I sewed bags for oak chips that we left in for flavor over the next few months. When we funneled our final product into the glass, we had a hundred bottles.

Our first harvest was exciting, but the work with the vines was never-ending. I went out into the vineyard with a water bottle, a hat, and pruning shears most weekends. I rationalized that since I was on-call anyway I might as well be productive.

Obstetrics often took the wind out of my sails; there were many sleepless nights and long days at the office. And at home, when I wasn't helping with the vineyard, I was feeding horses, chickens, cats, and dogs or tending to the garden. Degrees in Veterinary Medicine and Horticulture would have come in handy. I was constantly thumbing through The Merck Manual and The Western Gardener.

Then one sublime day, Pancho came to the farm to work, and my whole life turned around. He was so quiet and serious when I first met him that I wondered if he spoke any English at all. He had a classically handsome face with an aquiline nose, a beautifully clipped mustache, and pale green eyes. His gregarious brother Ben, who was part of the crew building our wine house, told us that Pancho had moved from Mexico to America ten years ago and had been working in the bean fields around Dove Creek. I got him to smile that day by speaking some Spanish, but I never got more than one word answers.

We bought a used house trailer from Ben, who also traded autos in his spare time, and Pancho moved in with his wife, daughter, and son. Within a month, they had invited us to dinner, and we were across the farm eating enchiladas rojas in plastic chairs crowded around a tiny table.

Pancho loved the farm, loved the work, and did it much better than either of us could have dreamed of doing. He had been raised on a ranch outside Chihuahua, and there was no plant or animal he didn't solidly understand. He quickly had the dogs trained not to bark, the horses trained to eat together out of one bin, and, somehow, the chickens trained not to steal their grain. John often tried to imitate his Spanish 'No' with the horses to no avail.

Pancho and I soon developed a special relationship to commiserate about John's vagaries; like planting rows of poplars between the fields so the farm would look like France. John was so adorable in those days that it was impossible not to love him, but some of his ideas were preposterous. He would outline the most outlandish plan, and Pancho would glance in my direction and say "We can do it." with a smile. I was simply glad 'we' was him and not me for the foreseeable future.

In the early spring of 1999, Pancho, John, and I met at the Cortez Sale Barn for a green chile stew lunch. We wandered over to watch the auction; and before I knew it, they had bought a sorry bunch of Navajo sheep and a couple of goats to boot. We took them back to the farm which had woefully inadequate fencing. They escaped on the second day, joined a cattle-drive passing by on the canyon road, and ended up in Utah.

The cowboy brought them all back in his trailer late that evening, and they looked exhausted. We kept giggling at his description of their little feet flying as they struggled to keep up with the cows in the back of the line. We were sitting in the half-light of the shed. It shone out on the animals in the field who hadn't raised their heads from eating or moved more than a few feet since we let them out of his trailer.

John turned to Pancho; "We need to get some sheep fencing up and make sure that they can't get under it."

"Okeedoke, what fields do you want me to fence?"

"All of them."

"Okay." Pancho nodded thoughtfully

"I've also been thinking that we need to make some duck ponds of our own at the bottom next to Wesley's."

"He said we could hunt on his ponds indefinitely. Do we really need our own?" It didn't seem high priority to me.

"I could take the tractor down there and build up some dams, but then we'd have to call my brother Ben. We'd need a bigger tractor to carry a ditch from the creek to where you want the ponds." Pancho was puzzlingly more enthusiastic about this than the sheep fence.

"Do we really need the ponds?" I wasn't convinced.

"Yeah, I want my own St. James's Park. It'll be easier to take people hunting, and Pancho and I can shoot ducks there too. Right Pancho?"

"We can do it."

We built our own duck ponds, but they were mostly used by the dogs for swimming. Jessie, our Labrador-mix from Shiprock, was gun-shy and too stupid to retrieve anything, but she loved to swim. You could watch her motoring across the ponds like a beaver. The ducks never moved from Wesley's. I don't know why John thought that they would.

16

MY PRACTICE WAS THE GOOSE THAT LAID THE GOLDEN EGG. In the end, the money was worth the nights without sleep as they didn't seem to do me any permanent harm. With Obstetrics, I always knew how many deliveries I had months ahead of time, and the surgeries and office visits were an added bonus.

I tried to give up Obstetrics after Pancho arrived, but Gynecology was definitely more tenuous. The Gynecologic procedures, like hysterectomies and laparoscopies, were generally booked and performed within the same month, so it was difficult to feel secure. And the office visits paid so little that they didn't even figure into the mix.

John would ask how many surgical cases I had for the week, and I sometimes overestimated to make him feel less anxious, then ended up feeling more anxious myself. I decided to deliver babies again within a few months because worrying about money was more stressful than going without sleep.

As a doctor, I had always been in a bigger town or part of a bigger system, so I never realized how prominent I would be as a the only Obstetrician in small community. I quickly came to the conclusion that, even if I wasn't drinking, I could no longer be seen at the Hollywood Bar. It was an authentic old saloon with a neon sign, pool tables, and a poker room in the back; definitely not for doctors. A perk was that I was never stopped for speeding. In no time at all, every policeman recognized my car.

I also stopped going to any small rodeos. I was the only doctor in the indoor arena at the Ute Mountain Roundup one night and watched the first man being thrown about like a rag doll on the bull's back. I saw one of the EMS crew look back at me and told John that we had to leave because I knew nothing about Orthopedics.

After a only a few years in practice, I was a respected member of the community. I had finally figured out how to answer 'Who operay?', but 'What's your opinion about the hospital?' was new and daunting. We, as physicians, became involved when the Cortez hospital had fairly serious trouble a few years after I got there, and I agreed to meet one of the County Commissioners at my office to discuss our perspective.

Joann, my secretary, rounded the corner with her eyes bulging and said, "We'd better get more chairs."

"Why, there's plenty of room."

"No, there's not, all three County Commissioners are here."

They filed in and sat down for an hour to hear my version of what was going on. Each time I started to answer question, I felt like I was pretending to be an adult for the first few seconds.

Being on-call was the biggest challenge of my medical career; especially with solo Obstetrics. All my clothes had to have pockets, so I could have the cellphone with me at all times; and each night I made a pile of clothes beside the bed, so I could change quickly in the dark. The exhaustion from going without sleep got worse as I got older, and it took at least three times as long to recover in my forties as it had in my twenties.

As the years passed, I also increasingly resented the restrictions. I never got to be carefree like the rest of the world at night or on the weekends. I was the kid who never went out and was left behind to do homework while everyone else went to the party. I'm sure I bored John with the weight of my responsibility because I certainly bored myself.

I remember his amazement one night, as we were eating dinner at a new restaurant in Cortez, when I ordered and vacuumed down two glasses of wine.

He said, "What are you doing? I haven't seen you do that for three years."

"I don't have anyone due, and I can't stand it one more second."

I stopped at two, but yearned for another, and fortunately got no calls to do a C-section later that evening. I scared myself with my wantonness; it was a non-repeated performance.

There was some compensation for being up in the middle of the night. It was magical to be alone in the dark in every season and travel the lonely road up the canyon in all kinds of weather. I would pass by the simple houses, see lights on in various rooms, and think about who was awake and what they were doing, I knew that Emma across the road got up around four and the Wings, from the Ute tribe, stayed up past two most nights. I pictured Emma making coffee in her tiny wooden shack and the Wings on the sofa watching videos, since they checked out six at a time from Citimarket.

I even learned the constellations from a fifth grade astrology book because the patterns in the night sky caught my eye. Sleepily driving the fourteen miles down the canyon road, I often felt like I was the only person awake on earth, and the stars were familiar and reassuring once I knew their names.

17

MY PARENTS AND MY SISTER CALLIE CAME for the harvest in September of 1999. When we knew what day the grapes were going to be ready, we also invited assorted friends and hired a few workers. On that Saturday, the canyon looked as beautiful as I had ever seen it.

My parents gave up picking after the first two rows. I made them iced tea and put them in the bottom floor of the tower which was the coolest place in either of the houses.

"It's awfully hot out there." My mother hadn't spent a lot of her life outdoors. She mopped her face with a dishtowel.

Daddy chimed in, laughing but partially serious. "I'm making a list of the things you need. So far, it's air-conditioning, an ice-maker, a clothes dryer, and a grocery store nearby. How long does it take you to get to town, and how often does it snow here?" He played with our newest addition, a Rottweiller puppy that had wandered up to the farm when she was six pounds and now was half-grown at sixty. I named her Laura, and she was a compact black bullet. She pulled at the dishtowel; he pulled back and matched the noise of her growling.

"It takes about thirty minutes, and it snows a lot. I'm pretty good at driving on it now." I took a turn with the towel. Laura lost interest because I wasn't growling.

"It's beautiful here darling, but I could never live in a place this remote. The West seems to be in vogue after that movie 'Dances with Wolves'. I've been reading that more of the jet-set have houses out here now." Mom's color looked a little less puce as she was speaking.

"This isn't Jackson Hole or Santa Fe. It's on the edge of the Indian Reservations."

Daddy was getting restless, "I know, that's why you don't have a grocery store. Where's the nearest place to buy a paper?" I gave him directions to the nearest gas station thirty minutes away to buy a newspaper.

I then arranged a comfortable place for my mother to read. She asked with feigned innocence, "Well, wasn't that movie about the Indians? You were never very interested in them before."

"It came out after we moved here." I shook my head and went back into my house to work on the food.

The sun streamed through the kitchen window and the sharp smell of the ham cooking made my stomach growl as I sliced the tomatoes from my garden, arranged them on a Mexican platter, and scattered basil and arugula on top. Callie dropped by to ask if I needed help with the food, but I sent her out to enjoy the day instead of employing her skills as a caterer.

The 'vintage', which John insisted on pronouncing with a French accent, was a tense day of the year. I was in charge of food, and the meal was the reward for our assorted friends who came to pick, but I loved the sensuality of the cooking and the solitude in the midst of the madness. Everything but the ham was straight from my kitchen garden, so I hoped it would make up for John's slave driving and the heat. I already had an impression of who was going to feel taken advantage of and not come back next year.

As I laid the plates heaped with food on the table, I got a glimpse of Pancho driving the four-wheeler through the nearest row of vines. The trailer behind was loaded with buckets full of grapes. I knew they would be finished with the front vineyards quickly. Daddy got back from the store, and I heard my mother exclaim with delight at the sight of the newspaper through the screened windows next door. I took the pitchers of lemonade and minted tea from the refrigerator and made room for them on the crowded table.

When I went out to find John and let him know I was ready, he was easy to track. I heard him talking as soon as I opened the door and stepped over the dogs sleeping in the sun. I gave him the signal without even having to interrupt his conversation.

The top of the peach cobbler was brown and glistening when I took it out of the oven. I tasted the whipped cream mixed with maple syrup, and it was so delicious I couldn't resist another try. Our best friend, Bertrand, had arrived early this morning with a crew from his restaurant 'La Marmot' in Telluride to help us pick. He laughed and pointed when he came in for lunch and found me guiltily licking the spoon. He was a rugged, fit fifty-five year old with a tall athletic frame. He had a look in his blue eyes which assured me that he also saw the ridiculous side of this 'vintage.' He and the two chefs bantered in French filling my kitchen with beautiful sound.

People filed in, filled their plates, and settled on the porch in the dappled light thrown by the cottonwood shade roof. The pickers this year were the usual exotic mix. There were silent Navajos from down the canyon who ate together in one corner without smiling, Mexican hands recruited by Pancho from a trailer park who loaded their plates with only ham, uncomfortable ranchers' sons who never looked up, and the Europeans and Telluride restaurant crowd who were totally at home. We had two tables full this year plus the ones settled on the ground, so I hoped we would finish before dusk.

The dogs perked up when they smelled the ham but were too polite to beg. Laura followed the smallest children around, and her nose unbalanced more than one plate. Callie and I ate in the kitchen and kept the table stocked with food. My parents were seated in the shade and being professionally social outside. I saw my father pour himself a tumbler full of wine. Bertrand was charming my mother, who watched his handsome face intently.

John was in his element. His sandy hair and eyes were the same color as his Carharts, and his face was brown from the sun. He made overly humble comments about the wine from last year, as it was poured, and feigned delight when everyone commented on how good it was. He stood to make a toast, and everyone looked up. He grinned innocently, showing off his dimples, and visibly swallowed hard in a boyish gesture before speaking. He turned on his English charm to thank the pickers for picking, me for the meal, and the gods for the vintage. He then rather abruptly announced that we should get back to work.

I told Callie that I didn't want any help cleaning up either and sent her up to take a shower. As I organized and washed the myriad dishes, I watched my parents on the porch through the kitchen window. They were still a handsome couple. Daddy poured the last of the wine into their glasses, and they both lit a final cigarette. My mother continued to look too warm, even under her straw hat. She sat primly on the picnic bench brushing away flies with irritated gestures. My father sat across from her and seemed oblivious to his surroundings. Every now and then he fed Laura a piece of leftover cheese or ham.

One of the French chefs who came with Bertrand said I must have grown up on a farm. I was certain he couldn't have realized that the two older people were my parents. They looked so incongruous there. They had lived their whole lives in Gaffney, a mill town in the upper part of South Carolina. My mother's family set great store by their participation in the American Revolution and Civil War. My father's family didn't keep track and ran the local jewelry store. I was uncomfortable in my Southern skin and rejected my mother saying that we were Southern first and American second. I don't remember exactly when the racism in the South became so abhorrent to me, but I do remember once exclaiming as a child, 'Look at those colored ladies' and having mother quietly explain that there was no such thing a a colored lady, there were only colored women.

I had come out west to get away from all that; it was Woody Guthrie come to life for me. Now my mother accused me of living here because the movie 'Dances with Wolves' was fashionable. I reminded myself that I had spent a good part of my life trying to please my mother with very little success. And it was preposterous; my life was anything but fashionable. Whenever I complained about losing touch with the modern world. John told me that the act of going out to dinner took no effort and was something one could resume at any time, whereas growing, butchering and cooking dinner were real skills. I had definitely become more adept at plucking a chicken, skinning a rabbit, pruning an orchard, setting a garden, and canning tomatoes. But milking Pancho's cow was not so easy; I could always sense the dread in her face when she saw me coming.

John and I both loved our life and the work together on the farm had made us inseparable, but the vineyard seemed to have changed something. It brought more and more people from the outside world, and John catered to them all.

The wicker basket creaked as I balanced it on my hip to go outside and hang the clothes to dry. I marveled at the pale yellow sheets fluttering against the cloudless blue sky and listened to the rhythm of the grapes being processed. Tables, buckets, and vats were brimming with the heavy purplish-blue clusters in a country scene that looked as old as time itself. Pancho caught me watching him and a serene smile flashed across his face. I waved, he laughed, and then earnestly returned his attention to the tasks at hand.

18

THAT FALL OF 1999, we put up enough grapes to make 1000 bottles of Merlot. We gave it our name--'Sutcliffe Vineyards'--because most of the other Colorado vineyards were named for their locations. We lacked the forklifts and bigger pumps needed to handle the volume properly, so the work to make wine was harder than it should have been.

We had, at least, invested in a crusher/stemmer, which efficiently spit out individual grapes ready for fermentation. For the first couple of weeks afterwards, Pancho and John stood precariously perched on the edge of the plastic vats and pushed grape skins down into the yeasty liquid with snow shovels every four hours. John fell in at one point, and we had to retrieve his sock. When the fermentation was completed, it was time to press the grapes.

The night of the press seemed endless; delivering a baby would have been easier. We bucketed the mixture into the bladder press by hand and waited a good thirty minutes for the water in the bladder to build up enough pressure to push the juice out. Our next hurdle was using the primitive pump to get the new wine from the collection container below the press into the stainless steel for storage. The smallest seed could clog the pump and stall the procedure, so much of the time was spent cursing.

Pancho drove the tractor into the wine house to remove the pounds of skins and seeds left behind in the press. We shoveled the heavy red solids into the bucket and created a gigantic mess by spilling lots onto the floor. Pancho dumped them in a corner of the nearest pasture and made several trips in the dark before it was all over.

We finished the whole process from beginning to end for two more batches and went to bed at four. The horses found the piles of fermented skins and seeds and were drunk when we got up later that morning. We moved them to another field; they walked with reluctant, staggering steps.

There was enough wine to age in four barrels, which was quite exciting. We used French oak and frequented the wine house over the following weeks, so we could smell and admire them.

I resolved to give up Obstetrics once and for all in the year 2000. I had done it solo for five years at that point and missed only a handful of births. I was glad my deliveries were few and far between because it was a snowy winter. Driving fourteen miles on the narrow canyon road with snow, ice, and deadly drops on either side had always made me hold my breath; regardless of what I told my father.

We decided to fly to Oaxaca for Christmas and the turn of the century, in the hopes that Mexico would not be fazed by Y2K. As we boarded, we watched the Mexicana flight attendant check our names off the list with a pencil. We knew any computer hiccups would be irrelevant in any case.

Oaxaca had a Christmas festival with radish sculptures that was famous all over Mexico. I was, at first, amused by the absurdity and then paralyzed by the poverty. The first day I watched the Zapatistas quietly bathing their small children in tubs outside the tents they set up on the plaza, but what I didn't realize was how many indigenous families were wandering the streets without food or shelter.

When I looked out of the sixth floor window of our hotel on Christmas morning, I saw three large families, with old people and children, huddled in the doorways where they had slept overnight. The trip was over for me at that point. I stayed in the room and ate very little. I wasn't even able to buy more than a wooden salad bowl to boost their economy.

I returned home with a commitment to learn Spanish and to try to help somehow. My disquiet faded as the days of the new century progressed. It was a wet spring, and I alternated my rides and walks between the Ute mountain and the National Monument across the street celebrating my new-found freedom.

My six dogs all came with me on the walks, but with Sam and Beth both over ten, I worried more about the distance. Laura was game for anything, even as a puppy; and Dusty, Jessie, and Max seemed pretty energetic. We found deep caves with remnants of cowboy things like old cigar boxes left inside, painted Anasazi ruins, jackrabbits, deer, and fields full of desert lilies in the far reaches of the National Monument.

I usually rode on the Ute Mountain, but my horse, Sage, was also beginning to show her years. Her dappled coat was still a burnished gold when she shed out in the spring, but she was close to twenty and I could feel the strain as she tried to oblige my every whim . She was so well-behaved that she never needed a bit in her mouth. If we saw one another from across the fields, the horse and I gravitated towards each other like magnets. I brushed her with my bare hands, pulled her mane and tail, and sat on her back as she grazed. She felt so much a part of me that I couldn't imagine what I would do without her.

19

THE SMALL OAK TABLE NEAR MY KITCHEN was the indoor attraction for all our guests. The house was in the shape of a cross, and that table was as close as you could get to the center downstairs; upstairs, the eaves formed a star where they met in the middle. If you sat facing South, there was a window that looked out on the first row of vines, only a few feet away, with the Ute Mountain rising up behind them. If you faced West, there was an adobe fireplace and a window that looked out onto the Battlerock. To the North, the house was a blaze of color. The bright yellow walls and over-painted red wainscoat led down the hall to our bubblegum pink bedroom. And, my kitchen, to the East, was dominated by a dark red tiled floor and old pie safes and cupboards in all shades of green.

I got back to the house one day from the red sands of the National Monument to find toothless Glenn Nash and John, in matching Carhart farm attire, sitting at the kitchen table having a cup of tea. John inflicted tea on everyone who entered the door; even Pancho's afternoons were centered around it now.

I was annoyed to find Glenn there. He had been a constant fixture at my house because he was welding the struts for our new hay barn, and he was ten parts talk to one part work. John settled into a similar pattern when Glenn was around, and I was tired of watching Pancho struggle to get the work done while they idled and shot the breeze.

"Well, well. Hello Princess." Glenn always called me 'Princess.' I didn't know if it was a positive or a negative thing.

"Hello Glenn. How are the mules doing?"

"Bonnie still likes to take on and off my hat. Clyde is getting fatter by the day."

"Tell Emily the story about the lizard! Wait, let me get Pancho." John called Pancho in from pruning the vines to hear the tale.

Glenn basked in the attention and settled in for a story.

"Did you know you could rope lizards?" I squinted in disbelief.

"You can, you know. They can't see that well in front of them, so you can hold fishing line right over their faces and slip it across their necks before they know what's happened. I roped one of those big blue ones, see. And put him in a cage and named him Larry. He was pretty good size and he got pretty tame, so I made a little leather harness for him. I used to take him to the Hollywood and have him pull things around the bar. He couldn't pull a whole beer, but he could pretty near do a half."

"And what happened to him?" I wondered why the folks in the canyon were so fascinated with large reptiles.

"He died after a couple of years. It was okay because it was getting harder and harder to find him flies." Glenn's voice tailed off.

I shook my head and realized that I was expecting a more dramatic ending or to find out it was a joke. I was never sure what I thought of the people down the canyon or what they thought of me. And the theater of our existence was only exacerbated by John's romanticism.

I was reading Proust that year and struggling with the idea that I had ditched my childhood and forgotten all my 'Madeline' moments. When I tried to call up memories, they seemed banal. I vividly remembered huddling in a wet bathing suit, smelling of chlorine, on a step outside the door to a room at the Gaffney Country Club. It was curiously named 'The Shibui Room'.

We weren't allowed to knock on the door of this hallowed, dark, air-conditioned bar where most of our parents spent all day drinking. Our only hope of getting enough money for the vending machines by the pool was that someone might exit, in a gust of air conditioning, to play golf or tennis. Since we also weren't allowed to enter, we could plead for a word with our parents at the door and were occasionally given some quarters if we promised not to bother them again. I wondered if the taste of the Coke with the whole narrow packet of Lay's peanuts emptied into the bottom would transcend time and reunite me with my childhood. I also wondered if I had any interest in where it might take me.

I worried that I had reinvented myself time and time again since I had left Gaffney. My accent was so thoroughly British at the end of my two years there that I was asked by an American how long I had been in this country on my return. It took nearly a month for it to disappear, and I didn't know whether to feel ashamed of being affected or proud of being so completely adaptable.

In an effort not to seem any sillier to myself in the West, I assiduously avoided cowboy hats, turquoise jewelry, and undershot heel boots. But I wanted to fit in somewhere, and I wasn't sure that being a doctor in Cortez was enough to convince my patients or myself that I belonged.

I was raised, in part, by a woman who was named Teacola after her two favorite beverages. The painful memory of her Mason jar and pie plate, in the broom closet next to the cleaning supplies, had always stayed with me. It seemed inexplicable that she made our food and washed our china, but she wasn't allowed to use it herself.

I liked Cortez, Colorado, in particular, because nothing was private. The field hands and the ranchers all sat down to eat together at midday. The schools, golf courses, swimming pools, parks, neighborhoods, and town meetings were all public. No one was embarrassed to stand up and voice their opinions at town hall; in fact, they rather enjoyed it. No patient called me anything but Emily (except the Navajo, who usually referred to me as 'Hey you').

We had made our life on the farm, but I felt disconnected from the people. They were evocative to me and we had the flow of life in the West in common, but it wasn't enough to bridge the gap.

That July 4th, I sat in my office and watched the horses and riders line up, as they waited to get onto Main Street for the parade.

Kierra, my nurse, came in and said, "Did you hear about that woman who died down the canyon?"

"No, where did she live? What happened?"

"It's that red house right before the Almon's. She was one of the First

Borns and delivered at home. I think it was her fourth. The placenta didn't come out, and she got infected. They don't believe in doctors, you know, so they just let her die."

"I could have removed it in five minutes. Did the baby do okay?"

"Yeah, now the husband's left with four small kids."

"What a pity."

There were quite a few religious sects in our neck of the woods, like the First Borns, who believed that God wanted them to do things the old way. We personally knew a similar canyon family down the road who buried three sons in the short time we were there. One of them died, when he was only a few months old, from a birth injury after a complicated delivery at home which was performed by the father. Another child was lost when one young son accidentally shot another while they were playing with an old gun that they found near the barn. The third died, as a young adult, in an accident with a motorized hang-glider.

John was often called out with the canyon men to dig graves in a plot by the one room schoolhouse. The graveyard was so primitive that it looked like the site of an Indian massacre in an old western movie. There were a few bunches of faded plastic flowers and small headstones with simple inscriptions of names and dates. They leaned in all directions in the sandy soil.

It was challenging to try to understand these people who were so different from the ones I was used to. It was as though they conspired to make life tougher than it had to be as a test of their willpower and ability to survive. And the conditions of the West were severe outside our irrigated enclave; the pitiless silence of the desert rang out harsh and true.

When I sat on my porch in the afternoons, I could hear the wind passing over the creek at the bottom before I felt it on my face. The ravens flew overhead, and I felt their dry rasping call and the whine of the air passing through their wings like it was part of myself. I waited in absolute silence, watching from the house, for the sun to touch the shoulder of the Ute Mountain each dawn and for the perfect shade of indigo to appear behind the Battlerock at dusk. As I crunched the pock-marked, cracked ground underfoot, I wondered how anything ever survived, much less prospered.

20

THE TERRACED VINEYARDS SURROUNDING THE HOUSES stretched from right outside our windows to McElmo Creek below. The grapes near the creek suffered most from the frost; the cold air seemed to hang down there. We were looking for a better place to plant an acre or two more when a physician friend of mine, Emily Lutken, bought the twenty acres above our eighty. Her land joined ours along its northwestern side.

John decided to do two things that worried me in the summer of 2000. We started construction on a house for Pancho and his family, and we prepared to finance and put in four acres of vines on the higher south-facing slopes of Emily's farm. Around the same time, I came home to find a shiny new orange Kubota tractor in the shed alongside the mossy looking John Deere. I didn't know what I was going to do to pay for it all.

I wasn't sure that Gynecology alone was going to be lucrative enough. I had a fair number of surgical cases scheduled, but nothing would have been lucrative enough at the rate John was spending. I had no other ideas about how to save more money either. I already wore my sister's hand-me-down clothes and shoes, which she sent in care boxes from Charleston, and shopped at the local thrift shop.

When I confronted him about it, John was angry and defensive and said that unless we enlarged, the vineyard would continue to be nothing more than a hobby. His arguments were fairly compelling. I did want Pancho and his family out of that cramped trailer, and we did need more vines and a better tractor to get to the next step. I argued that we didn't have to do it all so quickly, but it seemed it was already decided.

I tried recruiting more patients from Utah. One of my first cases from Monument Valley was a Navajo woman with uterine prolapse. I had to submit paperwork for two months to get approval from Utah Medicaid and wasn't entirely certain she understood the procedure because her friend and translator was monosyllabic in English and in Navajo.

I always worried when I used a translator because of a patient I had in Shiprock. She dutifully came to two preoperative visits, underwent a hysterectomy, spent three days in the hospital, and returned for the first postoperative visit. She was at her final check-up, and I commented to the daughter on how well her mother had done. The older woman, who had been good-natured and taciturn throughout, interrupted with an earnest question in Navajo. The daughter turned to me and said, "She wants to know exactly what you did and why you did it."

My Monument Valley patient proved to be more savvy than I expected, and all went well. But when I received payment from Utah Medicaid that barely covered the secretarial costs, I decided that expanding in that direction might not be the answer. I went back to covering almost all of the C-sections in Cortez at the expense of the little freedom I'd enjoyed. I was worried about satisfying our expanding debt, much less paying off any principle.

John was spending much more time in Durango and Telluride to market the wine. He had also found customers at Dunton Hot Springs; a fashionable ghost town on the back road to Telluride where they took exclusive guests. He loved the social aspect of selling the wine and was happy to be back in glamorous restaurants at night talking about his wine and the vineyard. When I remarked that I missed seeing him, he reminded me that we had lived for years around my schedule and now we would have to adjust to his. The problem was I didn't have anything that I could adjust.

I was back to no alcohol, no hiking, no riding with only the occasional day off. I couldn't ride anyway since my mare Sage's heart was failing. Gerald, our local Vet, had no doubt about the diagnosis when he saw her, but said we didn't have to put her down unless she stopped eating or couldn't get around anymore. The thought of her dying never left my mind for very long. I led her around to all her favorite eating spots on the weekends and cried and cried. She continued to have a good appetite and clearly didn't understand my grief or was too discreet to let me know.

The restrictions gave me one more chance to prove to myself that I could live simply and not be distracted by too many choices like everyone else in the modern world. And I loved the farm; it was hardly a prison. But I definitely needed more projects at home because I was going to be stuck there for a while; perhaps years...

I decided to try to get in shape once and for all. I had a Solarflex machine that I used once a week, but I stepped it up to four sessions weekly. It was on the top floor of the tower and was burning hot in the summer, but I hoped that might make it work better. I also promised myself that I would sprint to the top of the Battlerock at least once a week with the dogs. I had timed my ascent in the past and chose a target time of eight minutes.

More discipline was also required for me to start truly learning Spanish. I bought tapes to use while I exercised, much like Richard Gere in 'American Gigolo', and resolved to stop speaking to Pancho in English. This was hard because he used so many Chihuahuan colloquialisms that I couldn't understand him when he simply said hello; and he seemed equally puzzled by any Spanish that I was using. But unless I forced myself, I knew I would continue being lazy when I had a perfect opportunity for immersion at home.

I bought a piano, and the last time I had played was when I was sixteen. Huge swathes of time were sure to be necessary to get my music skills back again. I found a local instructor in Cortez and started weekly lessons.

And there was the garden, the bread baking, the canning, and millions of books I hadn't read. I told myself that my freedom would be restricted for only a few more years. After all, I was forty-two and had survived up until now. It was the first time I remember feeling that 'delayed gratification' was beginning to wear on me. There had been four years of college, four years of medical school, six years of training (counting the two in England), five years with the Indian Health Service, and five years of perma-call in Cortez. I longed for an endpoint because I had stopped believing in the light at the end of the tunnel. Coping with the tunnel had become a way of life.

21

THE SUMMER WAS DRY and passed by slowly, so I celebrated the rainy fall. My sleep was scented with the smell of wet sand and desert sage. Field mushrooms began to push up through the dirt between the grape rows, and we ate them in soups and stews. I had a taste for the more exotic ones from the high mountains and called Bertrand because he was the best at finding them. We arranged to go foraging on a Sunday, so I told the hospital that I couldn't take call for a few hours around midday.

The night before the appointed Sunday, I heard Pancho drive down in the four-wheeler. It worked its way into one of my dreams, and I woke up hours later in the half-light at six. John had driven to Napa for equipment, right after we picked the grapes, and the harvest was in full force. My leaving for the day meant that Pancho would be handling the fruit on his own, but I decided to go anyway because I missed Bertrand and wanted to get out on the hills before the snow claimed them for the winter.

It had been ten years since the first time that I met Bertrand. John and I went to his restaurant in Telluride to have dinner when we were living in Shiprock. La Marmot was known as the best restaurant in town, but that didn't stop us from arriving at eight on a Saturday night to see if we could get a table. We talked to him at the bar for two hours and finally sat down to eat at ten. He joined us for dinner and for our lives thereafter.

Bertrand pursued skiing all over the world before settling down with a French restaurant in Telluride. His family still lived in Paris and sent young French chefs to work as apprentices in his kitchen in the summers. I heard he was the most beautiful skier on the mountain, but refused the lessons that he offered me. A resistance to playing in cold snow was the only thing Southern about me.

Bertrand and I shared tastes in art, music, literature, and almost everything else. He taught me to climb mountains, cook French food, find mushrooms, and slow down and enjoy life. He was the older brother I had always wanted; my older brother, Joe, still lived in my hometown, and we had nothing in common.

Bertrand's wife, Noelle, was an avid gardener, and she was a fanatic horse lover. She grew vegetables for the restaurant on a farm they had north of Telluride and raised horses, cows, pigs, and sheep like her family had in the Vosges. Her flower beds had splashes of primary color like those of Monet, her horses were immaculate, and she was practical and rooted. They didn't spend much time together, because she wasn't interested in leaving the farm and he wasn't interested in staying. His loves were skiing, hiking and travel; and when he wasn't playing, he was working in the restaurant in town.

I had volunteered to bring a picnic, so I went out to gather food from the farm. I took the eggs from the hen house for egg salad and picked cilantro and cherry tomatoes from the kitchen garden. I also snagged the ripe white peaches that I'd spotted on the tree outside my bedroom window in the early light.

I managed to pull it all together and get out of the house by nine. I waived guiltily to the dogs and Pancho as I wound down our dirt road under the cottonwoods leaving them all behind. My drive was unimpeded and skirted the most glorious part of the Rockies which looked even better in the morning sun.

We met at the entrance to Lizard Head Mountain. I was dismayed by all the horse trailers with orange streamers in the parking lot. I had forgotten it was the last weekend of the third rifle season; things weren't so pristine after all.

"Think we'll get shot?" We both, after all, were dressed in green and brown. He shook his head defiantly.

We pulled four grocery bags from his car, put our knives in our pockets, and wandered up the hill in a much more relaxed fashion than we would have in the beginning of a hike. We knew if our timing was right, we should find the cepe mushrooms before the worms set in and the chanterelle mushrooms in profusion. There was dappled light covering the forest floor, and the camp robber birds called to each other from high in the trees.

When I climbed mountains with Bertrand, we didn't waste too much breath talking on the way. But once we were on the summit, our words flew. Mushrooming followed a different, but similarly predictable, pattern. There was a lot of talking in the beginning, and it always took forever to find the first mushroom.

The wandering got to the point of aimlessness that day. I was crossing a tiny creek behind when I heard him exclaim, "Voila!" In a clearing between the pine trees, vibrant patches of green moss carpeted the rocks, and the chanterelles crowded together and spilled down the hillside like knobs of gold.

His face was beaming, "Let's get to work."

We pulled out our knives, cut them near the base, and tossed them into the bags. We filled three bags each. The weight of them was gratifying as we struggled to carry them down the hill.

As a bonus, on the way out, we found a few cepe. The first one looked flawless; Bertrand spied its beautiful russet cap at the base of a tree. When he cut the stem from the cap, we saw the telltale tracks of worms in the base.

"You know they fall out when you dry them."

"And you know Americans don't eat worms like the French." I couldn't bear the thought of a little dried worm staying behind.

"What do you think is in the worm?"

"You have it then. I hope you enjoy the extra protein stuffed with mushroom"

Fortunately, we found two untouched ones for me.

It felt good to unload our bounty when we got back to the car. He brought out a beautiful Provencal tablecloth, and we sat on a small hillock which rose above the top meadows. We greedily ate our egg salad sandwiches, slurped down the peaches then turned our faces to the sun. I mentioned how I loved Camus, and Bertrand admitted he'd been unimpressed with him as a teenager. I was dumbfounded, especially since I was jealous that he'd been able to read him in French. He explained that he distrusted the dignity that Camus and the Existentialists found in suicide and thought it was an extreme stance. Bertrand loved life way too much to ever contemplate exiting it of his own accord.

We giggled as some hunters encased in bright orange emerged from the trees and then got up to go. He took most of the mushrooms to his restaurant. I anticipated the first taste of mine cooked with cream for supper.

It was dark when I got home, and Pancho had already fed the dogs. The night sky looked so close that I lingered on the porch for a while. There was a fingernail moon, the air was crystal clear, and the Milky Way transected the farm with the Dippers behind and the cat's eyes of Scorpio hanging over the mountain in front. I went inside, poured myself a glass of Sutcliffe Merlot, melted some butter in a pan on the stove, and started cleaning the chanterelles.

22

THE HAY FILLED THE NEW HAY BARN THAT FALL, and the cottonwood trees were a stripe of lemon yellow across the creek. The grape harvest had been our biggest yet. We hoped to double the year before and make at least two thousand bottles of wine. This time it would be Merlot, Syrah, and Cabernet Franc. I collected grape leaves in all shades of orange, red, and yellow and pressed them in stacks of my old Physician Desk Reference books.

Bertrand returned from a trip to California with friends in tow; the pigs needed butchering, so Noelle had stayed at home. When I picked up the phone on the Friday after he got back, he enthusiastically informed me that he was bringing the Californians by the farm over the weekend since they were driving right by it on their way to a camping trip in the Utah desert. I feigned delight but was not enthusiastic. I was trapped by call, so there was no chance of me escaping to hike in another direction.

Bertrand loved our farm better than he did his own. Our running joke, when he said he was coming to visit, was to guess how many people he would bring with him. It was flattering to watch him show off the place and know that he considered it his second home. He brought all different sorts of people through: his staff, visitors from France and Argentina (where he had a vineyard in the past), olympic skiers, and film industry executives from his restaurant days in L.A. But it could become annoying when I was not expecting it.

All in all, I was not that great at rolling with the punches during those years. John said it was because Americans were less hospitable than Europeans, but I thought it was more likely that I was exhausted so much of the time from lack of sleep. And I was always anxious that I could get called to a C-section or the Emergency Room in the middle of cooking, making beds, or doing laundry. I often returned to a houseful of people and didn't even know which meal came next. As I drove up, I would see them lounging under the cottonwood branches and grape arbors which shaded the porches and find the door of the mud room wide open with my six dogs wandering in and out of the kitchen.

So, like the majority of my weekends, I was stuck on the farm with a five minute tether to my car in order to be at the hospital and ready to operate in thirty minutes if there was a call for an emergency C-section. When I explained things like this to Bertrand, he would ask, 'So what happens if you have a flat tire on the way?' John had remained so uninterested over the past seventeen years that he only grasped that C-sections and ectopics meant imminent departure.

Sunday morning, when they were due to arrive, I resorted to my usual tactics and gathered up the dogs for a walk. I took a container of water, some peanuts and some raisins, and headed off with my book across the creek. I told John to say that I was on the hill with the dogs, if anyone asked. I found a spot where I could see, but the dogs couldn't, so they didn't bark at the guests. I was camouflaged on the first shelf of the Ute Mountain by the tops of the cottonwoods that grew by the creek at the bottom. My car was close in case I got called for an emergency, and I could see both houses through the fluttering yellow leaves.

They came late. I had already been an hour in the sun by the time everyone arrived. I considered myself ridiculous. I was forty-two years old and hiding like I did when I was ten; maybe my parents had been too tolerant of anti-social behavior. John seemed to bask in the admiration that people felt for the beauty of the farm and for us because we built it. He boasted to me that we had created something like Winston Churchill's Blenheim Palace in the wilderness; a destination. I wondered if I hadn't created a monster.

I looked at the faithful dogs around my feet. It was hard for all of them to lie in what little shade was available from the scrappy junipers and pinions near-by. They were aging so much more rapidly than me that it was startling. My stamina on the hills had improved while theirs was visibly waning. It broke my heart.

I had five of them with me, Fortunately, Sam was in the comfort of the house. At thirteen, he could barely make it to the edge of the nearest field, but still managed a swim in the irrigation pond before dinner when it was hot.

I could hear Bertrand talking in the distance. His English was unintelligible due to a combination of a soft palate injury from radiation as a child and his Parisian accent. I understood everything he said, but most people couldn't. I knew he was probably gently insulting the Californians, and I wasn't even there to get the joke. I loved Bertrand, but when he brought guests, I wasn't as interested in seeing him. By the end of my work week, I was tired of talking; and it seemed that's when the farm was just cranking up. Lately, there was the addition of the multi-national group from Dunton Hot Springs. My house often felt like something in between a Wild West outpost of the United Nations and EuroDisney.

After three hours of sitting, I was thirsty and hot, but determined that I could wait them out and thought I saw signs of departure. I chanced walking in the tree cover by the creek to see the horses. Sage came over to put her nose in my hand. She had continued to eat through her illness, but moved around so slowly that most of the time I let her roam free where ever she wanted. Every now and then, I would hear the clip-clop of her hooves and look up to see her wander on the porch outside the kitchen window. I usually had some treat handy; a pear or an apple. If not, I picked clumps of alfalfa from the field across the fence, which stained my hands green and made her nicker with happiness.

I heard a car door slam and waited for a few more. When all was quiet, I wandered back up to the house. John relayed that Bertrand was sorry to have missed me and brought a book that he left as a gift. The Californians were apparently very enthusiastic and had taken lots of pictures. He also said Christopher, a British artist visiting Dunton, had called and was coming to spend a night next weekend. I inwardly groaned and started washing the mountain of dishes.

23

"THE MAN WITHOUT QUALITIES' by Robert Musil was the book that Bertrand gave me. I was so impressed by it that I memorized whole passages and carefully wrote some others in a blue journal following the ones from Proust. I particularly loved his irreverence and praise of the irrational. Musil postulated that man's greatness was rooted in irrational thought and that the rational conscious mind was driven to become increasingly mediocre by the influence of commonplace ideas. I had a love-hate relationship with irrational behavior, which was much like my one with the South. The South that I remembered was entirely irrational.

My great-great grandfather fired the first shot of the Civil War and had a military college diploma from the Sovereign State of South Carolina. As children, we were taken to the island that our family inhabited, more than one hundred years before, to mourn the disintegrating tabby buildings and gravestones, which marked the passing of the South. From the time I was four, I could identify and avoid Yankee Foods like potatoes, carrots, and beef in favor of tomatoes, rice, and pork.

We were brought up to abhor ostentatious displays of money that bespoke of carpetbaggers and applaud breaking any rules, even the laws. Southern sons were regularly congratulated on their skirmishes with the police. Being wholesome was also equated with being Northern; smoking and drinking were patriotic in the South.

We lived in a split level house in a suburb of a town full of rednecks; yet I was given a list of Charleston last names suitable to marry when I came of age. I was allowed to walk downtown barefoot in nylon dresses along the railroad tracks, then was sent to a boarding school at age fifteen where we could never go without shoes.

My mother refused to go to the Episcopal Church in Gaffney when they removed the 'Thee's' and the 'Thou's', and too many mill people showed up. And my father was the president of the association which formed the first private school in Gaffney, which, not so mysteriously, coincided with the year desegregation occurred.

Mom taught chemistry at the local college, and my father had a wholesale jewelry business. It operated out of the basement of the house that we lived in. There were deep safes full of jewels downstairs and burglar alarms that went off when you opened a door or a window. I was shown the locations of hidden push-buttons to call the police, and there were guns around every corner. We also usually had a couple of Airedales in case everything else failed.

My parents led a life that centered around the start of drinking at five each afternoon. My brother and sister are six and eight years older than I; and as the youngest child, I was largely ignored. My parents were tired of raising children, so I ended up spending a lot of time with the dogs. There were photographs of me draped across them before I could even walk. They slept in my room at night, and I held a running monologue with them anytime I was awake.

I grew up by myself. I set my alarm in the morning, showered, and carefully chose my clothes. In the kitchen, I poured the milk on my Instant Breakfast to let it dissolve while I got my lunch ready. After school, I would make triscuit and tuna canapes and retire to my room to watch TV. 'The Brady Bunch', 'Dark Shadows', and 'Leave it to Beaver' were my particular favorites.

When I was twelve, my brother got arrested for selling LSD. As a result, my father became interested in drugs and carefully researched marijuana. By the time I was thirteen, my entire family smoked pot, grew their own stash, and pontificated about how drugs should be legal. I was never to join them; it was my act of rebellion.

My mother started adding the occasional Quaalude to her nightly Scotches and Librium. My father schizophrenically embraced smoking, drinking, drugs, and health food. I reluctantly swallowed cupfuls of vitamins, tablespoons of seawater, and droppers of dilute Hydrogen Peroxide.

At age fourteen, I started trading the Phenobarbital, which I took for seizures three times daily, to my brother for Eric Clapton and Neil Young albums. I was so depressed from the combination of puberty and downers that I was reduced to sitting in a darkened room and listening to Simon and Garfunkel's 'Sound of Silence.' At fifteen, I decided to take myself off of them altogether, independent of any advice from my parents or the doctors. The withdrawal was difficult, but worth every agonizing moment spent trembling in bed. Fortunately, my seizures were going away by then of their own accord.

Being average or 'common' and following the herd had been discouraged throughout my life by my snobby, intellectual mother. Any reverence I had for authority was deconstructed by my father whose dictum was, 'Laws were made to be broken.' Irrational was all I had left.

Life with John was certainly not average, but I worried that in my latest permutation as a round-the-clock doctor, I was losing touch with my rebellious soul. Musil's philosophy illustrated that I was being good without enthusiasm and drearily paying my dues. It made me ponder how I had arrived at that juncture and question whether my life was the one I had in mind.

My life had worked for sixteen years despite all my family's misgivings. It had been expansive and daring without any petty concerns or regard for personal comfort. The problem was that I had begun to sense that I continued being uncomfortable just to test myself in small ways that didn't matter. No one was going to care that I had no air conditioning, no clothes dryer, no dishwasher, no ice, and not enough water to flush the toilets regularly, or that I was suffering from no freedom from work, no help with guests, no privacy, and inflated expectations of flawless performance. I wondered if I had lost sight of the big things that mattered to me and not taken the exciting risks to do something that really made a difference. But I remained a willing and happy martyr in any circumstance.

24

LATE ONE AFTERNOON IN THE EARLY SPRING OF 2001, John called the office to let me know he'd shot my horse. He said that she got stuck in the creek, and her stomach was so swollen from the heart problem that it was impossible to get her out. It was the easiest way. I wondered if he was trying to conform to the heartless image of the Old West that might not exist anywhere outside the canyon anymore.

Sage was the first horse that had been mine alone. I could jump on her and gallop bareback around the farm or swing a saddle on her for the surrounding hills. I used her as an armchair while she grazed, a bridge to cross the creek, a ladder to reach the apples on the trees. We went on huge jaunts, just the two of us. When I was riding, I loved to feel her sides trembling as she whinnied, her stomach growling, and her snorts to clear the dust from her nose. It was hard to believe she was gone.

I had to do a C-section after work and kept crying in the changing room. I didn't get home until around seven.

"So you shot her?"

"Right in between the eyes. I'm sure she didn't feel a thing."

"Are you sure she couldn't have gotten out?"

"Emily, you know how swollen she was. She was almost dead from exhaustion. She'd been struggling to get out for hours before we found her. It was the quickest way to end her suffering."

"But she was still standing up?"

"Yes, it's the hardest thing I've ever done, but I did it for you. Pancho and I loaded her up into the truck and took her to that high mesa a few miles down the road. I wanted to have it all done by the time you got home."

"Thanks, I know you did the right thing, but it's still hard."

"I know, I remember when I lost my first horse." He put his arm around me and patted my shoulder.

My tears were involuntary and fell like rain. I cried when I looked out the dining room window at her favorite clump of grass under the Russian olive tree or let my gaze wander across the creek to the hill where she would stand, looking precariously balanced, on the mud cliffs at the base of the Ute Mountain. I walked down by her favorite grove of trees and could still see her sheltering there. I buried my face in the flanks of the other two horses to drown myself in their smell, but they didn't smell like Sage. Pancho cried with me. Every time he saw me, his eyes welled up.

John had some magic around horses; it was the sexiest thing about him. I glowed with pride when he compared me to a 'good mare' when we first started dating. He played polo in those days, and the sight of him galloping across the fields used to make my heart stop. I would lead the winded horses away after each chukker and curse him for riding them too hard, but I marveled at his skill.

He gave me a young Arabian mare instead of an engagement ring; and, as we lived in New York and she was unbroken, I never got on her back. I didn't have the heart to ask what happened to her in later years or demand a present in exchange. I finally did get to spend plenty of time on horseback when we moved out West. John tolerated my fearfulness and lack of experience, but was frustrated by my lack of bravado. It was a standing joke that I was a 'gutless swine' when it came to bad trails or riding new horses.

When Pancho came to the farm, his horse skills put John to shame. I learned from him how to stand quietly with them and how to watch their behavior. He taught me what tone of voice to use and how to wait for them to ask to be caught instead of catching them. I was able to achieve equanimity with them on the ground; on their backs, it was a different story.

I had been pursuing wild horses on the Ute Mountain ever since we bought the farm. I ran across their tracks, on the other side of the fence, leading up a narrow cliff in a place that was impossible for even the best cowboy. I then tracked them every time I crossed illegally into Ute Territory. The males left their scat in only one place, so there were stud piles as high as my waist. I could see where they rolled and the tiny footprints of the foals, but I never caught up with them in the flesh. Fear kept them enough distance away, and their eyes were much better than mine.

Gene said when he was a boy, they caught wild horses down the canyon. He swore that when they were broken to ride, they were the smartest horses around. He told tales of trapping them at the bottom of an impassible cliff then roping and dragging them back to the farm with a person in front and behind.

We went to the wild horse round up in Moab, and most of them seemed only a little bigger than Beth, my German Shepherd. It was amazing to watch the cowboys balance on the bars of the high fence above them to drop a halter on their nose; it reminded me of Glenn's story with the lizards. Once they were tied, it was palpable when the horse shivered as it felt the first touch of a human hand on its flank. I knew that if I ever ran into the ones I was chasing, a glimpse would be all that I would get.

I was grateful that I'd known a horse as fine as Sage and hoped her spirit would still hover above the places that we loved the most; the sand that we galloped down in the dry bed of West Rock Creek, the mesa-top in the National Monument where we always stopped to see the farm and she whinnied to her friends across the street, and the shade under the old cottonwood tree where I pulled her saddle and we would both nap: she, standing on three legs, hanging a foot, and I, with my back up against the trunk, in a state of absolute contentment and peace.

25

A COUPLE OF MONTHS AFTER SAGE DIED, John bought a buckskin paint horse named Wally from a friend who was moving to town. They posed both of his children, under five, on his bare back, outside my picture window. He had a calm nature and was easy to manage most of the time, but he was not as willing as Sage. I accepted that I might never find another horse like her and enjoyed him as much as I could.

I was half-asleep listening to my two roosters crowing when I heard a big rig pull up followed by an insistent knocking at the door. I pulled on my jeans and opened it to find Clarence Stash smiling as fresh as a daisy.

"You said you wanted to start early."

"I know Clarence, but maybe not quite this early. Come on in, I'll put on the coffee."

"John awake?"

"Are you kidding?"

"I'm going to go unload the horses first."

"I think we cleared out four corrals. Need help?"

"No." Said like he's never heard anything more ridiculous.

Clarence Stash was one of the Filfred cousins from a notorious family originally called Mustache; a name left over from the trader nicknames, like 'curly', for features the Navajo would never have. He was part Hopi, part Navajo and spoke English with a bemused smile and the oddest Native American accent I'd ever heard. He stood about five foot three, and his face had been reconstructed from severe burns when he fell in the fire as a child. I had never seen him wear anything but a faded western shirt, jeans, and cowboy boots.

He was poetry on a horse and used to ride bulls in the rodeo. His family was rumored to thieve horses and cattle on the reservation, but aside from picking up the occasional wandering mule, Clarence floated above it all. Unlike us, he believed in what was seen and unseen. When I ran into three bucks on the highest point of the Battlerock, he said that they were Navajo spirits watching over me.

Clarence and John had cooked up a plan a few months ago to explore Canyon de Chelley on horses. It was the most sacred Navajo site, and Clarence had registered to be our personal guide. It was hard for me to believe that it was actually happening.

The coffee smelled strong and encouraging. I heated a saucepan of milk, preheated the stove for biscuits, and transferred my homemade plum and apricot jams from the Kerr jars into small white bowls. I then tiptoed across the porch into the tower and timidly called upstairs to Christopher to let him know Clarence was here.

Christopher dropped into our lives after coming down from Dunton to spend the weekend that previous fall. He seemed to find something he was searching for in the ordinary rhythms of the farm. He was pretty lovable, so I didn't protest too much. He was quietly hip, over six feet tall, and athletic and graceful. He had a shaved head and the most beautiful green eyes; you could watch emotions moving across them like ripples on the water. Christopher and Clarence had become fast friends. They made an odd couple, a tall British artist and a short Navajo cowboy. They would nod and smile at the horizon when they sat together on the porch, but didn't exchange too many words.

As I passed by the kitchen garden on the way back to the house, I noticed all the herbs; parsley, mint, thyme, sorrel, and tarragon, were returning. The arugula had kept producing all winter, defying logic, and was taking over half of the garden. John was awake and pottering around the kitchen in his bathrobe by the time I got back. He smiled, gave me a peck on the cheek, and ate a spoonful of the apricot jam before the biscuits. Christopher appeared in the same grey T-shirt, army fatigues, and tennis shoes as the night before, I called Pancho in from outside, and put the kettle on for tea.

In the background, I heard the footfalls of the horses getting off the trailer and the occasional whinny from ours who were in the large fields down by the creek. I hoped that Pancho hadn't already fed them, so they would stay waiting on the fence line until after breakfast.

While the biscuits were in the oven, I went to the mud room and threw my saddle, blanket, and snaffle bit out onto the porch. I figured I had just enough time to see what horses Clarence had brought, so I wandered over to the corrals. In the first stall, I recognized a horse we had traded to him. His name was Skunk, because when he ran he lifted his tail in the air. In the second, inexplicably, was my horse, my Sage, an identical buckskin mare only a little taller and a lot younger. I ran back into the kitchen, and Clarence was beaming. "Well, what do you think?"

"I thought it was my horse. She's her double!"

"It is your horse. She's come back to you. I looked all over the Reservation and found her." I gave him a big hug and a kiss, which made him visibly uncomfortable.

Her name was Buttercup, which Pancho interpreted as Butterfly, so we decided to call her Mariposa. I was slightly disappointed because I was still riding Wally; she wasn't 'finished' enough yet. But when I went down to bring him up from the bottom, he seemed happy to see me and eagerly put his nose in the halter; mostly because he wanted to torment the new horses. I led him, Handsome, and Cholo, the naughty thoroughbred that Christopher liked to ride, up to the top. I scolded them all for pulling along the way.

We arrived mid-afternoon at Canyon de Chelley; and after lengthy discussion with the Navajo authorities, got the permit for two days. The first ride started at the bottom. We bumped the rig along down the winding dirt road, parked, unloaded, saddled up, and took off. The horses were interested and animated. We were dwarfed by majestic red cliffs on either side and trotted in and out of shallow water which ran over rusty colored sand. Aside from Sage being absent, it was perfect. There were ancient dwellings high above in the red cliff walls, huge petroglyphs, and meandering side channels. Clarence rode my new mare; she seemed responsive and intelligent. Wally was much better-behaved than I anticipated he would be.

We returned to the trailer at sunset, and the whole world was red; light, rocks, sand, water. Clarence was unbelievably strict about brushing out the horses and checking their feet, and they seemed to like the attention. It took almost one entire motel room to store the tack; there was a huge pile of aromatic leather as you walked in Clarence's door. After a dinner of Navajo frybread and mutton stew in the motel dining room, we collapsed with the most delicious exhaustion.

The second day, we decided to ride to Spider Rock, the birthplace of the Navajo people. This time we were starting from the top of the canyon. This proved quite a challenge for John and Clarence because Christopher was afraid of heights and I was afraid of everything. The path was narrow, poorly kept, and full of huge boulders. Wally literally hopped from rock to rock, but proved to be amazingly sure-footed. It was so terrifying that I couldn't even speak until we reached the bottom.

We found a beautiful, well-kept Navajo farm around the base of the spire and were taking pictures next to one of the fences when a sweet teenaged boy came out of the hogan and asked if we wanted to get closer. As we were exploring and posing inside the fence, he threw only a blanket on his horse and galloped away up the trail we had just descended. He reappeared at the bottom after only a few minutes holding something. He shyly handed it to me and said, "You dropped a glove."

26

MONTICELLO, UTAH WAS A SMALL TOWN that sat under a mountain with the face of a horse naturally etched out in trees on one side of it. It had a hospital that just stayed alive by taking chronic care cases as a permanent nursing facility. The head nurse had approached me about doing some outreach surgery at the hospital when I was still doing Obstetrics, but it was an hour away and impossible. In the meantime, I had stopped Obstetrics; and a Family Practitioner named Karen, with some surgical experience, had come to Cortez. I was able to train her to do C-sections, and she had been helping me with call. In the late summer, the administrator in Monticello contacted me again, and I decided to talk with them to increase my case load and pay off some of the debt.

During the drive, I felt guilty about the fate of small hospitals in today's rough economic climate and the forty plus miles local people would have to travel if Monticello shut down. When I arrived, Leander, the administrator and a guy with a camera were waiting for me at the front door. I looked at them quizzically.

Leander said, "I know you haven't decided if you're going to do surgery here yet, but we thought you might, so we've invited the newspaper. We're just so excited that you're coming to look" He beamed like a politician.

"I'm seriously considering it." I said.

"Well, if it would be alright with you, he'd like to take the pictures and interview you for the story. He can throw it all away if you change your mind." He motioned me inside the front door.

"Sure." I nodded and thought that this must be a sleepy town.

Needless to say, I succumbed. This was more complicated than it seemed for quite a few reasons. First, there was the drive; an hour back and forth on a road that was, more often than not, snowy in the winter. Second, I needed to set up clinics, schedule surgeries, and when I operated, I had to stay in a local motel until the patient was discharged from the hospital because of the distance. This meant three days a month away from the farm at the very least. Third, although there was no visible difference, the culture gap felt more pronounced than with the canyon families or Native Americans; the town was solidly Mormon.

The Mormons were a new phenomenon to me when I moved out West, but then so were the Californians. The first Californian I met was a Family Practitioner named Bob in Shiprock. I thought he must be wildly religious because he seemed so incredibly happy and realized later that he was not overly religious and was truly happy; his charmed life in California had left its mark.

The situation with the Mormons was the one I was suspicious of at first with Bob. Salt Lake City radio regularly broadcasted that Utah was the state with the highest use of antidepressants in the nation. And there was a telltale Mormon accent which was more noticeable in the women. Because they talked with a fixed smile, their T's and S's were very accentuated. I was able to pick it up from a mile away and found it exhausting to watch them pretend to be so animated.

I applied for a Utah Medical license and hospital privileges in Monticello and spent the first weekend there in the fall. The 2001 harvest had been disappointing due to a late frost. We remembered the day that we lost most of the newly forming fruit because it was the morning of June 3rd; John's birthday. We had a vintner from Napa staying with us for the week, and he was saddened to tell us the extent of the damage. He also told me that the beautiful colors in the grape leaves, that so enchanted me, were due to a virus.

I settled into the Monticello Days Inn and pulled out my reading material. I unpacked the can of beans, my cereal, and the bread and put them on top of the tiny microwave that was stacked on the refrigerator. I put the cheese, oranges, and bag of lettuce inside. The room was dark. Paintings of Southern dogwoods and azaleas hung over the two beds and looked as out of place as I was. Through the small windows, I could see the golden angel Moroni on the spire of the white temple to the left; the mountain was straight ahead in the distance. I wondered if I could find my way up to the trees that formed the lower part of the horse's head next summer.

I missed my dogs, I missed my kitchen, I missed John. I mindlessly rearranged my things on the long counter next to the TV. I planned to use the monastic environment to read the books that were more difficult for me to understand. Wittgenstein was put to one side for early morning when my mind was clearer.

At the bottom of my suitcase, I found my 1998 copy of 'Diversions', which I had searched for and included as inspiration. There were many magazines that came unsolicited to doctors' offices. Most were about clinical issues, but 'Diversions' was unapologetically about consumer goods for the doctor; vacations, wines, restaurants, cars... that is, most of the time. They did a special issue in 1998 that I'm sure provoked more dreams than all the previous ones put together. It was called 'Doctors who Volunteer'. Almost everyone I knew saved that copy and thumbed through it with good intention from time to time. It had a directory of organizations around the world and made volunteering seem like it was simply a phone call away.

When I was in my third year of residency, I wrote to Unicef and WHO with thoughts of providing medical care in a needy country after I finished. I received short standard replies. Both required a masters in public health in addition to my medical degree. During the years in England, I applied for a job in Burkina Faso and met with an official at the Kenyan embassy in a quest to help in Africa. Again, I found that I didn't have the correct qualifications.

I was quite excited in Shiprock when a breast feeding project that I did with the Navajo brought the Johns Hopkins foreign aid team to my doorstep, but nothing came of that either. In Cortez, I contacted Doctors without Borders, but they wanted more time than I had at my disposal.

I decided to try harder. I couldn't go through my whole career and not do the thing that interested me the most. Volunteering to give medical care to those in need could not be impossible. I felt perfectly prepared by my trials and tribulations. I had adapted to a foreign system of health care in England, worked with a different culture and language (albeit, with translators) on the reservation, and coped with having no back-up in Cortez. In Monticello, there was not even a surgeon to fall back on. If I had trouble in the O.R., I was on my own. I was also learning Spanish, which would open up almost all of the Americas.

But then 'learning' might have been an overstatement. There were a few things I had figured out, but it was hard to know if they were peculiar to Mexico or general rules:

> 1.) Always subtract any -*ito* at the end of a word, and you might get to something you understand.
> 2.) *Mande?* was more polite than *Que?* if, as usual, you don't understand a word of what's been said.
> 3.) If someone invites you to a party then says, 'I'll see you at *tu casa'*, it didn't mean they were having the party at your house. 'Mi casa was tu casa' in perpetuity.
> 4.) *Que padre* had nothing to do with who your father was; it was an expression for 'cool'
> 5.) One should never say *Tengo huevos*, because it was boasting; even if, male or female, you did have *cahones*.
> 6.) *El comio la torta* with a knowing expression had nothing to do with having eaten the sandwich. Instead, it had everything to do with pregnancy before marriage.

These puzzles remained:

> 1.) Why were there 60 year old *Senoritas* with wedding rings on?
> 2.) Why did Pancho and I still call each other *Usted?*

I did, however, learn a new expression from one of my patients which was the most beautiful one I had heard. The Spanish words for birth were *Dar a Luz*: To Give to the Light.

27

FOR TEN YEARS, ALMOST EVERY TIME WE HAD A VACATION, John and I would pack up the car and drive down to Mexico. We became so blasé about it that once we had to turn back an hour and a half into the trip because we had forgotten our passports. Our routes varied; we crossed in Nogales, Juarez, and Douglas depending on our destination. We would explore the countryside for days and days. I knew the states of the Mexico much better than I did the American ones; having never ventured over or up to Wyoming, Idaho, Oregon, or Washington.

We were seasoned drivers of the back roads and toll roads. We had faced buses head-on, experienced near-misses with animals at night, almost run out of unleaded gas, and been searched by truckloads of policemen with machine guns. Shortly after Pancho came to work for us, he became obsessed with us making a trip down to meet his parents and see his hometown of Nonoava in Chihuahua. As plans progressed, it became evident that there would be no one left to run the farm if we all went down together, so we decided on a two week road trip with his brother Ben, leaving Pancho behind to mind the fort. When they heard we were going in November, Christopher and Bertrand eagerly decided to join us.

I thought a road trip to Mexico with four of my favorite men in a Dodge Ram truck with a camper shell would be my idea of heaven. The border crossing in Las Palomas, next to Juarez, was fast and easy; and we drove past endless one-street towns seeing only a few people hanging out by their cars in front of colorful cement facades.

We spent the night in Cuauhtemoc; a town full of Mennonites who still wore the same clothes as when they moved to Mexico in the early 1900s and were famous for making cheese. John and Bertrand had their first argument, over a delicious breakfast of huevos rancheros and rolls called bolillos, the next morning.

Ben, Pancho's brother, was talking about the narco-traffic in his hometown and Bertrand said, "The power and antics of Spain and the United States are the cause of Mexico's corruption."

John jerked his head up, "You've been talking to too many people from Berkeley. Mexico is the cause of Mexico's corruption. The Aztec were corrupt long before Spain hit the scene."

"And the Spanish played into it and used it to their advantage just like the United States with their Banana Republics all over Central and South America."

"I suppose the rich and powerful are responsible for all the trouble in the world... and everything else for that matter. You and your Berkeley crowd have a point there; you just haven't considered what sorry shape we'd be in without them."

"I don't see them doing such a stellar job." Bertrand had stopped eating.

"You are just like the Mexicans that receive their help. You suck up to them in your restaurant then snipe behind their backs when they've gone." Christopher and I stared down at our plates. I couldn't look at Bertrand or Ben after John's remark. Ben leaned over and whispered in my ear, "What does 'Berkeley' mean?"

I escaped to the back of the truck and stretched out on the air mattress by myself for the rest of the morning. I watched Mexico stream past; it felt like being on a train.

We turned from the highway onto a primitive dirt road that wound for hours over rocks, up and down hillsides, and through rivers. When we finally arrived at the house, Pancho and Ben's parents were sitting outside on the stoop. It looked like they had been waiting there for hours.

Their mother gave me a warm hug and had a charming smile. She'd cultivated a beautiful arbor of vines shading a mixed garden of flowers and vegetables between the modest house and the stables. Their father was tall and imposing. He barked out polite commands that John, Christopher, and

I couldn't understand. Bertrand, who was fluent in Spanish, spent most of his time flirting with their twenty year old sister Ana, and we were largely silent. I was sad to find that my comprehension was abysmal. Christopher watched everything with a serene smile, and John occasionally gestured and spoke too loudly to try to communicate.

In the mornings, we walked across to the stable where the calf was tied and cranky after the long night, milked the mother, let him loose, and watched him run greedily to the teat. Then we carried the milk across to the house and put it in our coffee while it was still warm. In the afternoons, I sat with their father under the arbor sorting out dried beans. It felt like playing an ancient board game with three piles; stones, shriveled beans, and good ones.

We stayed for three days and were fed fabulous meals with endless handmade tortillas piled in the center of the table. The women never sat down to eat with us, so it was me and the men at the table. After supper, Ben's father disappeared behind a colorful curtain to watch cartoons and laughed so loudly that we'd all start laughing with him in the kitchen. The last night, I finally convinced his mother to sit down beside me at the table after dinner, and she silently took my hand in both of hers and lovingly patted it in her lap.

We left Ben behind and drove down as far as Zacatecas. My afternoons there were spent alone reading in a park full of white lilies and noisy grackles. Political disagreements continued to surface between Bertrand and John over dinner on a nightly basis. Christopher received a call and seemed relieved that he had to return to New York early. Bertrand, John, and I decided to head back to the border by way of a town named Creel in another part of the Copper Canyon; there was very little conversation on the drive.

John and I had never managed to find our way deep into the Copper Canyon on previous trips, so we decided to hire a guide to get us to the bottom. We had also only glimpsed the native Tarahumara people in the distance before they hid in the trees. The guide took us to a hanging ladder, which ate up a quarter of the distance down the side of the canyon; and he knew the Tarahumara families, so they came out when he yelled for them with a few small wares. They were the most fascinating people I had ever seen. They were short and sinewy with matted hair and colorful clothes. They seemed untouched by the modern world and made me feel like a visitor from another planet when they stared up at me. The guide told us that they still hunted down animals and killed them with their bare hands. One of the men demonstrated his skill with a slingshot, and his whole family ran inside for shelter. We nervously stood in the open wondering how rude it would be to join them.

We picked up a tourist book in Creel on the way back to the hotel, and it had information about a free clinic that had been set up for the Tarahumara and was run by the Jesuits. I found the white building on a deserted square littered with blown plastic bags and peered in the barred windows. I felt so alone. The silence of the square, late on a Sunday, was palpable; I could imagine it transformed with laughter and conversation Monday morning. The waiting room had plastic chairs in scattered patterns and a small opening in the crude cement wall for reception. It looked functional and earnest; as though the medicine that really mattered was practiced inside. It was what I had been chasing my entire medical career. I decided, however impractically, to try to work there in the future. Political arguments didn't appeal to me, but trying to make a difference, even if it was just with a few people, did.

28

IT WAS IMPOSSIBLE TO BE IN MEXICO without thinking and talking politics, and Bertrand drove John crazy by defending positions that seemed paternalistic and apologetic. He said that developing nations had limitations which precluded them from progress; John thought that they should be held accountable for their futures. Bertrand found their greed and crimes predictable given their circumstances; John thought everyone should be judged by the same standards. Bertrand said that first world investment in the developing world was fueled by exploitation; John thought it was the only way forward.

I stayed out of it because I knew that arguing with John was a no-win situation. He felt that he had been brilliantly educated by the British system and spent much of the day staying abreast of current events. He was clever, articulate, and extraordinarily well-informed. He could also be a bully.

In the Shiprock community of like-minds, I watched him tear into the kind-hearted Ivy League doctors with trepidation. He pointed out how convenient it was that the Native Americans were provided for them so they could feel good about themselves. He told them the primary purpose of the Indian Health Service was to create jobs for the Navajo on the Reservation and the medical care they provided was only secondary. The Anglo teachers who worked in the schools also got an earful. He said that the educational system with its non-reading graduates was disgraceful and Navajo as a first language was no excuse. His criticism of those who were doing their best to help might have been more convincing had he ever tried to help himself.

There were countless holes in his theories that became more distressing to me the more I tried to ignore them. I particularly thought his stance on hard work and personal responsibility might have held more sway had I not entirely supported him for the past thirteen years.

I was eager to know more about Ben and Pancho because they seemed much happier than most of the Americans I knew. I coveted their contentment and the lightness in their step. Both boys grew up without enough money for shoes or clothes; and both stopped school because the family couldn't afford books, pencils, or paper. Ben came to America when he was thirteen, quickly learned English, got a job in an orchard, and started sending money home. Pancho, who was younger, followed a few years later. Yet, there was an amazing lack of bitterness, which I found with most of the Mexicans I knew.

Pancho thought he'd had a charmed childhood; swimming in the river, fighting with the obstreperous donkey, milking the cow every morning, and walking barefoot in the desert. Ben took us to all their favorite places in Nonoava. He showed us the paths they were frightened to ride on, because ghosts dropped into the saddle behind you from the overhanging trees. He took us across a suspended bridge to a village where the mayor lived in a modernized cave. And he knew every edible plant and seed from wandering the countryside. We snacked on small grains inside rolled grasses, sucked on corn stalks, and chewed on leaves.

John and I weren't disconnected from the land. We explored the canyons and mountains around the farm together on foot and on horseback. We found nests full of duck eggs by the creek, picked wildflowers, and tracked the animals by the creek. We harvested the vegetables and fruit from seeds and trees that we'd planted and cared for our animals as a team. And after exhausting and fulfilling days, we walked down the road to the old apple tree and looked at the stars hand in hand. But my life with John was changing, and those moments were now few and far between.

29

NOT LONG AFTER WE RETURNED FROM MEXICO, our dog, Sam, died. I think Pancho was relieved that it happened after we got home. Sam had become incontinent, so we bought a large doggie bed that was easily washable and put him in the tower each night to sleep. On the night that he died, he ate a full dinner and settled down into his bed. When John checked on him the next morning, he was gone without any sign of struggle.

It was like losing my oldest child. I never thought of his death being sooner than mine when I first held him as a puppy who grunted and smelled of his mother's milk. We found him at a farm in Dorset, deep in Thomas Hardy country, and didn't get back home until dusk. We went into the field across the street, and he looked perplexed when we plopped him down in the grass. His black feet seemed as large as his head at that point.

"How are we ever going to house-train him?" I asked John.

"You have to show them."

"Show them what?"

John peed behind the cover of the hedgerow. Sam watched, squatted, and did exactly the same thing.

John smiled, "It works every time."

I loved Sam so much that it prompted me to collect more dogs to ease the pain when he died. I realized that it didn't lessen the pain at all; it just meant I would have to go through it six times instead of once. John and Pancho took him to the high mesa, where they left Sage's body, and found a deep cave that looked out on the Ute Mountain. They hoped to keep the large animals away by rolling a stone in front. I wanted to go and see the place, but I couldn't face seeing Sage. John said that parts of her body were strewn everywhere from the lion and coyotes.

The day after Sam died, I was hanging the clothes on the line, and the dogs came around my feet. They looked up at me with the oddest expressions on their faces; a mixture of questioning and sadness. I told them he was gone, just as I used to tell my rooster when he clucked worriedly over the body of a hen who'd just died. They may not have understood the English, but they seemed to understand my tears.

I wrote to the Jesuit priest in charge of the clinic in Creel offering my services when I returned (in English). I was pleasantly surprised that the letter got there and I received a response until I opened it. I basically got a 'Thanks, but no thanks. God bless you.' (in English). Thinking that it might be the family planning part of my specialty, I wrote back offering services which were not related to birth control. Again the letters travelled back and forth efficiently; and again I received 'No thanks, but God be with you.' Maybe I should have written it in Spanish. Maybe I got the 'Letter in English / No Money' standard reply. His correspondence did seem unrelated to my propositions.

I sat at my kitchen table on Christmas Eve thwarted again. The vines were an endless collection of sticks and wires in the winter, and the Ute Mountain was covered in snow in the distance. John tried to resist the commercialism of Christmas in America, so there were only a few Christmas cards dotted around and some juniper branches with homemade decorations. I was glad that we were going to Pancho's house that night for a drink, even if I couldn't have one because of call. With the children and the decorations and lights, it was a lot more festive.

Creel, Chihuahua would have been perfect; the Tarahumara needed help, and it was only a fifteen hour drive from the farm. I sensed that the priest probably wouldn't be any more malleable in person so I gave up on that specific location, but Mexico was fixed in my mind as the destination for my unwanted good will. All I needed to do was figure out how to make it happen.

I had no way of objectively examining my motives, but I thought I could be less subjective about my impressions, questions, and conclusions. I decided to make lists to keep my thoughts in order and to stop myself from getting lost behind the barriers and being defeated. I found an unused journal with a faded red morocco cover that John had given me for my birthday a few years ago. The paper was ruled in the center with wide margins making it perfect for lists, and there was a flap that folded over from the back to the front to close it. I wrote at the kitchen table as the light faded and the mountain turned pink with Alpenglow.

Things I was sure about:
The indigenous people were marginalized in Mexico.
They lived in remote areas.
They were distrustful of contact with anyone else.
They were living at a subsistence level.
They had local governments and leaders like the Navajo.
They still used traditional healers for the bulk of their illness.
There were a lot of children's graves in the graveyards.

Things I thought were true:
They were uneducated about sanitation and water sources.
They delivered most of their children at home.
They cooked over open fires in small, poorly ventilated rooms.
They had no refrigeration.
There was no catch-net of free care for the poor in Mexico.
They couldn't afford medical care.
There were some local clinics.
They were run by new doctors doing their year of social service.
They often didn't have medications on site.
There were no accurate health statistics.

Things I needed to find out:
How many foreign Non-Government Organizations were around.
Where they were located.
If I could work with one of them.
The requirements to be able work as a doctor in Mexico.

What standard medical practice was like in Mexico.

And if it was similar, just by osmosis, to the United States.

How receptive the medical community was to foreigners.

What diseases were around.

What standard vaccines everyone received.

If they followed World Health Organization Guidelines.

And if they did, how they implemented them in the remote areas.

This was clearly going to take the rest of my life. Bertrand told me that I was already taking care of an indigenous population in America, so I should simply try to be happy with what I was doing. But I felt I had the capacity to do more than that. I knew that if I left the Southwest, my varied patients might have to drive further or pay more, but they could still find medical care. I wanted to fill a bigger gap, and I had found a huge gaping hole.

30

IT WAS A UNSEASONABLY WARM DAY IN FEBRUARY of 2002, and I was kneeling in sheep poop and covered in blood. I had people showing up for lunch at my house in twenty minutes. We were three hours into it. Glenn, who had lots of experience with sheep, in addition to roping lizards, was already drinking at ten when we called him to see if he could help. He came armed with a six-pack and had polished off all of them. The dead lamb lay beside me in the straw, and my hand was deep inside the patient mother. I had already removed lots of chunks of placenta because it wouldn't separate on its own which Glenn assured me was common with premature births like these. The uterine wall felt mighty thin, even non-existent, in places. I decided it was the best I could do and took my hand out. Amazingly, she jumped to her feet, but all her bowels protruded out from behind. I told John to shoot her and ran back to the house. I heard the shot as I reached the kitchen door. Poor thing, she tried so hard; I tried so hard.

I switched on the burners and the stove on my way to the bathroom, peeled off the bloody clothes, and watched the rust-colored water disappear down the drain in the shower. I was definitely not in the mood for a party.

I stood aimlessly in the kitchen afterwards, fought back the tears, and tried to concentrate on the food. The slow-roasted chipotle pork was cooked and only needed warming up. I wrapped the tortillas in foil and tucked them next to it in the oven. The huge pot of black beans needed heating up on the top of the stove. And it would not take me long to make the salsa verde thanks to the cooked tomatillos and the blender. I was glad I decided on something as simple as ice cream for dessert and made the chocolate sauce and walnut cookies last night. I had absolutely no appetite. It could have been worse; we could have been having lamb.

The paper plates were garish red plastic, and the napkins looked like Kleenex. I felt guilty both about the environment and using them for the Dunton crowd, but I couldn't face another major wash-up and the aftermath of bath towels spread across the kitchen counters with precariously balanced glasses, pots and pans. I wondered how it would feel to have a full staff like they did in Dunton or at least a teenager to help with the dishes.

I heard the SUV's pull up and watched people flood onto my porch and admire the view of the Ute mountain with the vineyard nestled underneath. I hesitated for a moment in the kitchen feeling sad and like I didn't belong.

There was a British couple who were good friends of Christopher's and who had recently bought land in Dunton. Their names were Bella and David. She was tall, blonde, and athletic like a colt. He was dark and exotic looking. Then, there was the German couple who owned the ghost town; Katrin and Christoph. Katrin looked absolutely beautiful in her jodhpurs, and Christoph was wearing a shirt which was ravishingly pink. I would have felt underdressed were it not for Bella in an army jacket and David in what appeared to be a pajama top.

I overheard John telling them my sad tale as he joined them, and everyone ran in to give me a hug. I knew nothing was going to make me feel any better; I still wanted to crawl under the bed and hide.

Everyone raved about how delicious the food was, and they did eat an incredible amount. The few mouthfuls I had were okay, but I couldn't bring myself to eat the pork. I tried to get out of riding in the canyons across the street, but they all thought it might be therapeutic. I hauled my saddle onto the porch in the hopes that someone would tack the horses then got the kitchen in some semblance of working order.

Mariposa was still not 'finished enough', and I was beginning to wonder if she was ever going to be. Pancho was calm and careful on her back, and she still seemed to jump around a lot. I rode Wally who was as reluctant as I was. We lagged behind the others lost in silence.

My favorite paths seemed barren and harsh that day. East Rock Canyon fell away to the left looking steep and menacing, and the cliff ledges were covered with tortured bits of juniper and toppled rocks. The trail along the top alternated between stone shelves and patches of ice. The sand on the way back was littered with dead-looking plants and a few bitten-off spiny cactus.

When we got back to the house, I made tea and put the leftover cookies on a flowered plate. I feigned cheerfulness and patiently waited for everyone to leave, so I could be sad alone with no one watching.

"That was fun.", John said, oblivious, as usual

"I think I'm going to go lie down upstairs."

"Didn't you think it was fun?"

"I did, but I'm not really feeling better yet from this morning."

"Everybody ate a ton. You know Katrin and Christoph said they were envious of the quality of the life we lead. It's a real compliment coming from them. They could have anything they wanted."

"It is, but it's hard for me to put the two worlds together right now. I'm having trouble with what's real and what's not."

"It's unfair to decide they're not real just because they have money. They have the same problems in life as everyone else."

"They live on a different planet."

"No, they don't. They're people just like us."

"Well, right now, I'm thinking about dying sheep."

"They said we seemed like the perfect couple."

I nodded, went to the upstairs bedroom, closed the door, got in bed, and stared at the ceiling. I tried to imagine the ancient world with no printed word, no recorded music, and no photography; the houses quiet except for human voices and the occasional instrument, the places of work serious and bare, the churches awe-inspiring with their stained glass, dark paintings, resonant organs, sacred books, and sculpture. Everything was real and authentic except the odd person who mimicked someone else. I wondered if I would survive the modern onslaught of noise, words, and images and stay intact.

Our friends from Dunton were witty, interesting, and politically astute, and I enjoyed their company and adulation. But I felt I was playing a part for them as the only American in the crowd. I certainly could play the part of the only farmer with ease. I clucked like a chicken, told gory country stories, and sat on the floor with the dogs.

I was only sure that I was myself when there was no one else around. John required the same amount of performance as any other outsider. He laughingly gave me his 'never hungry, never cold, never tired' rule when we met, but I knew that he meant it and realized that any vulnerable parts of myself were unacceptable. It seemed to fit with his being English. I was punished for not having a stiff upper lip if I complained about circumstances or illness. And no bad days were allowed; not being cheerful was selfish. He often said that he didn't really know me and he was right, he didn't. I lived in my own private world just as I had when I was a child.

I was greedy for those moments when I was not trying to make everyone else happy. The animals were part of the answer to who I was when no one was watching, but even they seemed a burden at times. I could see sympathy and expectation in their eyes and wanted to make them happy too.

That night, I questioned the indifferent ceiling of the upstairs bedroom as I had so many times before. The bedroom was under the eaves, and I set it up to resemble Van Gogh's famous painting. There was a high bed covered with an old quilt, a yellow chair with a rush seat, and a couple of simple Dutch paintings. It was where both of us went when we weren't feeling well or couldn't sleep. The corner of the ceiling next to the garret window had no answers about who we were or why sheep died. The light slowly left the sky, and I fell asleep fully dressed and didn't wake until morning.

31

I FINALLY MANAGED TO WORK IN MEXICO early that summer with a group named Liga, otherwise known as The Flying Doctors of Mercy. They ran a clinic in a town called El Fuerte in Sinaloa, required almost nothing in the way of paperwork to volunteer, and the time commitment was only a weekend. That and the name should have forewarned me that they were a little more interested in the 'flying' than the 'mercy'. We drove down in our pick-up and found little of interest on the way except a dirty beach called Huatobampito where I insisted on swimming in the ocean despite the water being full of blue jellyfish. Miraculously, we didn't get stung.

El Fuerte was a bland, but pleasant, town with a majestic river running through it. We arrived a day early and checked into a fairly lavish hotel that Liga had recommended. It was a hundred and ten degrees outside, which made even short walks mind-numbing, so the air conditioning was a welcome relief. The next afternoon, we heard a roaring noise from inside the hotel; and the manager smiled knowingly and said, "They're coming." We went outside and saw six small planes on the horizon. The next thing we knew, 'they' had arrived. The group had good intentions, but they were disarmingly self-congratulatory.

The facility only functioned one day each month, except in the late summer months when it was closed altogether due to the heat. The doctors were gathered up primarily from L.A. They came with assorted interested others and as much equipment as they could fit in the planes. The number of patients mobbing the front of the building was staggering, the heat was stultifying, and the lack of patient privacy was discouraging. I was given a bowl of water to rinse my hands, one sheet of paper to use, again and again, for twenty patients, and a faint penlight for pelvic inspection. I asked about surgeries, and the last one they recalled was a tubal ligation with the medical student swatting flies in the O.R and a severe wound infection to follow.

I did the best I could, but was sad about the conditions, especially when I compared them to the amenities in the hotel. It wasn't as if running water, single rooms, and electricity were impossible. I was also disappointed that my Spanish was so woefully inadequate again. I sat in uncomfortable silence with the patients whenever the translator disappeared. We worked for only one day and primarily dispensed American drug samples. Despite all that, I came away even more convinced that setting up a clinic in Mexico was what I wanted to do, and I would try as hard as I could to overcome any obstacles.

Bertrand called a couple of nights after I got back.

"I'm in my restaurant, and the Creels are here."

"Someone from Creel?"

"No, the Creels!"

I thought I had lost my ability to understand Bertrand. "Creel is that town in the Copper Canyon where we stayed and where I tried to work."

"I know. These people are named Creel, and they're from Mexico."

"I don't necessarily see the connection."

"The town is named after their family, and they go there all the time. They're interested in your ideas about starting a clinic and know a lot of people in the government. His uncle is the Secretary of State. They'll be here through this weekend. Can you come up and meet them?"

"I'm covering C-section call because I just got back from Mexico. Any chance they could come down?"

"No, I think they have pretty full days of hiking planned."

"Be sure to get their names and contact information and give them mine."

"I will. They want to eat here every night." So, Bertrand was not so cynical about the idea of starting a free clinic in Mexico after all. He sounded more excited than I'd heard him in a while. I reconvened with my lists for analysis:

Things I was sure about:

The Mexican people were eager to have free medical care by
 foreigners.

This foundation had enough American interest and donations to
 survive.

The Mexican physicians were involved and receptive to collaborative
 care.

The physical plant and supplies could be easily improved.

More reliable charting and record keeping for statistics were
 imperative.

A clinic needed to function more than one day a month to be useful.

Things I thought were true:

American physicians could practice medicine in Mexico.

It was possible to cross the border with equipment and drug samples.

American doctors were also able to perform procedures in Mexico.

A connection through the Creels with the government couldn't
 hurt.

Standard medical procedure in Mexico and America was pretty
 similar.

The diseases were fairly similar as well.

Things I was unsure about:

How to get money.

Where to put the clinic.

Which physicians would be willing help me with it.

If my Spanish would ever be up to par.

One of the primary things that struck me while working with the
Indian Health Service was the sense of pride it gave the Native Americans
to know someone cared. I wanted to try to do the same thing for one of the
indigenous populations in Mexico because I could feel their marginalization
and isolation. I was certain they felt invisible at times.

The Tarahumara in Creel already had the Jesuit Clinic. Chiapas had
a large indigenous population, but also much interest, since the Zapatista
uprising, from the big organizations like Doctors Without Borders and

Doctors of the World. And Liga was working with the Yaquis in Sinaloa. We had been visiting a town in the state of Michoacan, called Patzcuaro, for the past twenty years. There were over a hundred thousand indigenous people in the area called the Purepecha who were unattended to. It seemed like the perfect place to put the clinic.

I enlisted two good friends. Emily Lutken lived on the hill above the farm. She had been my friend and colleague since the days in Shiprock. She was a Family Practice Physician and the most astute clinician I had ever seen. She had also done work in refugee camps in Afghanistan and Pakistan in the past. Jim Hanosh was a General Surgeon who had come to Cortez about the same time I had. We had assisted each other on many cases since 1995. He never imagined he would be helping with hysterectomies, C-sections, ovarian cysts, and fibroids. I certainly never imagined I would help with gallbladders, ruptured bowels, and colon resections.

Jim said he had a patient who wanted to donate money to a good medical cause in a developing country, so most of the things I was unsure about on my list seemed possible. My proficiency in Spanish might be another story.

32

THE ACCOUNTS RECEIVABLE FOR MY MEDICAL PRACTICE were always much larger than they should have been. I would set up payment plans with no interest for self-pay patients and accept as little as ten dollars a month on two thousand dollar bills. I managed to make the practice work for me financially over the years, but it was a mixed bag of returns. It was impossible to predict what you would get paid based on what you had billed. There were too many variables.

Medicare reimbursement (for those over sixty-five) was low, but uniform, and there was no quibbling about the plan of care. Medicaid reimbursement (for the poor) varied wildly from state to state, and I had to deal with four of them; Colorado, Arizona, Utah, and New Mexico. Utah was by far the worst; very few providers would have anything to do with patients covered by Utah Medicaid. I did, but it probably cost me money.

Insurance reimbursement was based on multipliers applied to the Medicare rates. The amount allowed for the same procedure varied with each insurance company and each individual's plan. And each company had their own seemingly senseless rules and regulations for precertification of procedures. I took any and all insurance, and there were more plans than I cared to think about. My secretary, Joann's, main job was to negotiate their nuances. I would only get involved if there was a problem, but there were often problems. I spent a lot of time trying to placate insurance company nurses who couldn't even pronounce the procedure they were refusing to pay for.

Then there were the self-pays; the Emergency Room call at three o'clock in the morning, the stat C-section, the difficult consult. Many of the calls in the middle of the night were for the uninsured who had postponed getting care until it was an emergency. We called them 'cases for Jesus' and expected no payment; although once I did get offered a llama for a D&C.

It all varied day to day, month to month, and year to year. The amount I was paid fluctuated from 55 to 72% of what I had billed, depending on the distribution and whims of the various component parts. It was a difficult way to run a business.

One of my worst business mistakes was made when our plumber wanted me to deliver his ninth child. He was a Mormon, had eight children from a previous marriage, and was on his first child with his new wife. She needed pregnancy care, and I had delivered her last child by someone else a few years before. I should have been suspicious when he made no payments during her prenatal course. After the delivery, he still made no effort to pay the bill, which was close to three thousand dollars. I heard he'd bought a new house; and since he was a friend, I told Joann to hold off on sending him to collection. I never saw a penny, and the next thing I knew he was bankrupt. He never even offered to do any work in exchange. It hurt my feelings when someone in town treated me like that. I ran into him at the July fourth parade the next year and was as embarrassed to see him as he was to see me.

It was a particularly hot August in the canyon in the summer of 2002. We had two weeks of temperatures over a hundred degrees without a hint of rain. The sun rose each morning like a relentless fiery ball, and I was on a run of call, so there was no escape. One Sunday, I decided to take the willing and able dogs to the top of the Battlerock; I put Beth, the oldest, in the house because she was so shaky on her legs. Laura, Jessie, and Dusty followed me unenthusiastically down our dirt road. Max had gone hunting and was nowhere to be found. We scrambled up the hot stony southern side. I had to lift Laura's hindquarters as her front claws clutched and scratched the rock above in the steep bits.

By the time I got to the top, I had a headache from the heat and exertion. The mesas stretched away to the West towards Monument Valley shimmering in the sun. The houses looked like tinker toys to the East with the silver ribbon of the creek winding round them. The dogs were panting in any shade they could find, so I didn't linger. We ran down to our favorite swimming spot, lay down in the muddy creek, and stared at each other in quiet relief.

Pancho yelled from the back porch of his house as we passed by on the way home. I wandered over and sat down in the shade. The most recent four acres of vines were planted right next to his house on Emily Lutken's land. They looked in perfect order. He teased me about swimming in the creek with the dogs, and his children came out and effortlessly changed language and cadence from Spanish to English and back again. We sipped agua fresca made with watermelon, salt, sugar, and lime. Nothing had ever tasted so good.

33

THERE WAS AN OLD MINING TOWN called Silverton that was ten thousand feet high and less than two hours away from the farm. It was lively for an hour or two in the middle of the day when the steam train discharged its passengers to buy funnel cakes and have old-time photographs taken in western dress. I tried to make a trip there at least once a summer, and I had convinced many to follow me over the years. It was the gateway to my favorite hiking trails; in particular, Highland Mary Lakes.

As a child, I thought the theme song and beginning scene of 'The Sound of Music' were mushy, unrealistic, and sentimental. But that was before I saw Highland Mary Lakes. Every time I went to this paradise in the high Rockies, I had to fight the urge to open my arms, run across the tundra, and break into song. I knew that if I did, even the deer would be embarrassed.

My trip this year included John, Bertrand, his son Julian, and Bella and David. We met early outside the POW, or Pride of the West bar, on Main Street. John and I abandoned our pick-up and piled in Bella and David's Suburban. Bertrand stayed in his car with Julian, whose sixteen years of age matched the time he'd been married to Noelle.

"So, we're going to an American version of Scotland? That town certainly didn't look Scottish. I did so want a funnel cake. I can't believe they're not open at seven in the morning." Bella had a penchant for anything fried in bad grease.

"The town is the Twilight Zone. If you spend the night, you can see drunk cowboys passed out at the tables in the POW with all those mounted animal heads staring down at them." I actually loved Silverton.

"It's sounding more like Scotland."

"Do you have funnel cakes?"

"No, we have haggis."

We crept up narrow switchbacks on the side of the mountain below the lakes. Bertrand's car, ahead of us, looked like it was going to fall off at various junctures. We stopped when we could go no further, got out, and started assembling our gear.

"Your lunch looks much better than our Skittles and KitKats. You're going to share, of course." Bella nudged Bertrand in the ribs. Her tousled blonde hair just touched her shoulders, and her blue eyes were so intense that they were blinding. He gave her a long smile and an affirmative reply. They had something major in common; he was an expert in flirting and so was she. In fact, I thought both John and Bertrand were in love with her, and I was jealous when Bertrand was enamored with someone. John was more of a flirt and less picky about women, so I'd been sharing him for years.

Bertrand was wearing shorts, and Bella noticed that his knee was swollen. When he showed it to me, I was alarmed by the size of it. He assured me that it didn't hurt. He'd had a skiing injury followed by an operation some years earlier, and since then had swelling from time to time.

"This much?"

"No, never quite this much, but I had a CT scan last week."

He promised he would let me know if it started to hurt; which, of course, he didn't. The walk to the top was no joke. There was a lot of coughing and panting from David in the rear, who had been trying to give up smoking for thirty years. Bertrand stayed in the back with him and never complained.

It was a perfect day. The lakes were still and mysterious, and the grass on the rolling hillsides surrounding them was a vibrant green; the light played deliciously off both of them. The last snow lay in thick mounds melting into the water, and the rocks were warm from the sun. Bella and David agreed it was exactly like Scotland after all.

We shared all the food between us and mused about the enticing crystal clear water and the temperature of glacial lakes. I walked into the water in all my clothes, felt myself go progressively numb from the feet up, and was still shocked when I summoned the courage to duck my head under. Bella, John, and David stripped off all their clothes, jumped off a rock, and came up gasping for air. Bertrand and Julian wisely abstained. I was the least wise of the bunch; especially since I had no other clothes. Bertrand gave me half of his, and we basked in the sun to dry off a little.

We walked a little further to Lost Lake in front of the rugged grey peaks of the Grenadier Mountains, and the afternoon clouds started to gather. Our descent was rapid to get to the treeline; more for protection against lightning than rain. We stopped for ice cream and Bella's funnel cake in Silverton, then followed each other on another terrifying road home. It was only open in the summer and consisted of gravel ledges, which crisscrossed down the mountainside. There was no way to remove the cars that had fallen off over the years, and we'd heard the story of every car that had slipped to join the others down below.

Bertrand and Julian went back to Telluride, so Bertrand could have his customary nap before the restaurant opened at five. The four of us went back to Bella and David's house in Dunton. The house looked like a converted barn with a huge black and white portrait of a bull along one wall and only glass at the far end framing the mountains.

John, David, and Bella went down to the ghost town to soak in the hot springs, and I stayed behind. I sat transfixed watching the light change and the clouds shift their position around the high peaks. It made me think of a quote that I loved from James Galvin's 'The Meadow': *The way people watch television while they eat—looking up to the TV and down to take a bite and back up—that's how Lyle watches the meadow out the south window while he eats his breakfast. He's hooked on the plot, doesn't want to miss anything. He looks out over the rim of his cup as he sips.*

34

BERTRAND CALLED FROM THE RESTAURANT a few nights after the hike and said they had read the CT scan and were asking him all the wrong questions. They asked if anyone in his family had a history of cancer. I remember exactly where I was standing in my bedroom when he said the word 'cancer'. I stared at the repeating pattern in the Moroccan rug in disbelief.

Then, for his sake, I tried to switch over to my doctor role and give him reassurance. I told him that it was impossible to know from just one CT scan of a swollen knee. He'd had knee surgery, the way things looked could be changed, so more tests needed to be done. I insisted that there was no way to be sure of anything until there was a positive biopsy and that scans were often over-read. And I had never even heard of cancer of the knee. In the end I almost believed myself, but I collapsed crying on the rug when I hung up the phone.

A week later, he called to say that he'd had a needle biopsy of the growth in his knee, and it was positive for cancer. I asked what kind of cancer it was, and he said they didn't know. It sounded so unusual that I still thought the diagnosis might not be correct. He had surgery scheduled for a larger biopsy the next week, so we held some final hope that it was all a mistake.

The resigned tone of his voice the next time on the phone told me that it wasn't. They had opened up his knee, assessed the extent of the encroachment, and looked at tissue biopsies. They still didn't know what kind of cancer it was, because the cells were so unusual, but they were sure it was a cancer. I encouraged him with success stories I had personally witnessed from combinations of chemotherapy and radiation, but it sounded hollow and sad to both of us. I made sure he was sleeping, not in pain, and hung up defeated.

I knew that the prognosis was not going to be good when I heard the cells were so unusual that they couldn't identify what kind of cell line the cancer started from; undifferentiated tumors tend to be much more aggressive. When Bertrand's total body CT scan showed spread to the lungs and several other places, I was dismayed, but not surprised. Doctors always say that only the nicest people get cancer, and Bertrand was no exception. He was kind and dignified, handsome and athletic; and he had cancer throughout his body. It was hard to think that his life was no longer under his control.

The thing that struck me the most about the many people that I'd seen with cancer over the years was how individual everyone's response to it was. Patients, doctors, nurses, family, and friends all responded to death being immanent and tangible in their own particular way. And there was no knowing which was the right way. There were aggressive doctors, ones who were the voice of doom, ones that believed hospice was the only solution. The wisdom I strove to remember was *the art of medicine is to heal the sick, comfort the dying, and not to get the two confused*. It was right up there with 'do no harm' for me.

Bertrand wanted to be aggressive with his cancer, and it was his decision to make. He had a radical surgery to remove the tumor from his leg at MD Anderson even though the cancer was already everywhere else. He recovered from the operation quickly, and the idea that he'd had it done seemed to make him feel better for a little while.

He then pursued the disease in his lungs with both radiation and chemotherapy; neither of which had much effect. I remember picking him up following a course of chemotherapy at a nearby hospital after he had lost all his hair and a lot of weight. He spent the night in the tower and couldn't keep down the water that I brought him, much less anything else.

John helped enormously with accompanying him to doctors and picking him up after treatments, but remained emotionally unaffected. It wasn't new, I hadn't seen him shed a tear in eighteen years, but I expected he would respond when something of this magnitude came along. When

I questioned him, he said he didn't care when people died and probably wouldn't even be sad if I died before him. He said, "When you're gone, you're gone; and when you mourn someone who's gone, you're being selfish."

Even if he had his emotions under total control, I still couldn't understand his lack of empathy for Bertrand's suffering. In retrospect, it fit with his lack of empathy for me every time I was sick or saddened. It seemed to make him angry instead of sympathetic. And I was so terribly sad, both for Bertrand's suffering and the fact that he was not going to be around for me forever. I realized the second part was totally selfish, but it was unstoppable.

35

MY NEXT STEP WITH THE MEXICO PROJECT was a reconnaissance mission to Patzcuaro. Christopher, David, and Bella were all interested in helping, so we headed down in the late fall. We flew into Guadalajara and stayed for a couple of days to avoid the crowds in Patzcuaro for the Day of the Dead on November first.

The Purepechan people had one of the most famous celebrations in Mexico. They made bread and candy in the shape of bones and skulls and brought toys for the children's graves and tequila for the adult ones. The graveyards were decorated with thousands of flowers, and the relatives stayed all night to tell their loved one's story to anyone who was interested. Guadalajara had no celebration at all. We asked for directions and walked to an empty graveyard at midnight which was a strange experience all round.

The next day, as we drove into Patzcuaro from Guadalajara, we passed a graveyard that I had never noticed before. It was so densely covered in woven wreaths and arches of marigolds, chrysanthemums, dahlias, and gladioli that it took my breath away. We brought the car to a screeching halt and walked inside. There were hundreds of candles and left-over remnants of fruit and food at each colorful memorial; and a striking number of children's graves. We saw one tiny mound marked on the corners with four slices of watermelon. The dates, disturbingly close together, were scribbled on a piece of cardboard at the head.

We stayed in an old hotel on the main square and hired a tour guide, even though John and I had been there dozens of times before. His name was Francisco, and he was eager to take us to the Purepechan towns to show us their crafts. There had been a Jesuit monk in the early sixteenth century who tried to create Thomas More's Utopia by teaching different skills in each indigenous town. Francisco had plans to take us to two of the towns where they made masks and copper goods. We puzzled him by asking to see the medical clinics and hospitals instead. He seemed unwilling until we threw in the traditional healers as well.

Our preliminary investigation confirmed that there was a need for medical care. The local hospital was over-flowing, and there were no other non-government organizations (NGO's) in the area. It also suggested that there might be more to the corunderas, or traditional healers, than we thought. There was one who had glowing green hands; either that or Bella and I both simultaneously imagined it.

Although the rainy season should have been over, it poured from dawn until dusk day after day. There were barefoot Purepechan women wading in rivers of water at the edge of the cobbled streets. We sat on the plaza under the portales and drank countless cups of hot chocolate. It gave us plenty of time to speculate and plan. We all wondered why, since setting up the clinic seemed like such a good idea, no one else from the United States was doing it. Doctors from the Unites States were traveling so far afield to do good work when there was real need in the country right on our border. One particularly rainy day, we cynically decided that the reason no one was helping in Patzcuaro might be the weather.

"David, can you take some shots of Emily while I buy a churro form that nice man we just passed." Bella had found the funnel cake equivalent in Mexico.

"I don't want my picture taken."

"That's tough, I'm going to write an article for Vogue. At least it will get us some attention. I doubt we'll get any money, but you never know. And we need to do an interview."

"Interview me? Can't you just make it up? You know all the answers." I wondered if John could take my place as the lead on the publicity part of the project, but I knew that since he wasn't a doctor, it wouldn't be very convincing.

"No." Bella headed back up the street

"You're going to have to get over this or you'll never be able to convince anyone to help you with funding. Just stoop down under that ledge and smile at John and Christopher." David sounded like a stern professor.

"If you promise to take only a couple."

I knew that fundraising was going to be the hardest part for me; and disappointingly, when we got back, we found out that Jim's patient wasn't going to be able to donate any money. Christoph and Katrin offered to help us get started instead; I was embarrassed, but excited to have them on board.

36

THE FOLLOWING WEEKEND, BERTRAND CAME DOWN to the farm with a couple of friends. He and I were sitting together over the remnants of a large breakfast at the kitchen table; everyone else had gone outside to pack the car. He got up, staggered, and immediately sat back down. For the first time, he let his guard down, looked at me, and said, "I don't think I can go on if it's going to be like this." I held his hand and said I was sure something could be done to make things better, but I wasn't sure at all.

He had a brain scan later that week which showed growth in the cancer that had spread there. The radiation dose to his lungs had been large, so I was relieved that he was able to have radiation to his brain, shrink the cancer, and continue to be able to walk.

Proust said: *To ask pity of our body is like discoursing in front of an octopus, for which our words can have no more meaning than the sound of the tides, and with which we should be appalled to find ourselves condemned to live.* I thought that most of us didn't realize we lived with that octopus until things went wrong; and even then, many were loathe to admit they had no control. Physicians were the worst offenders

For us, it underlined the fact that we didn't understand the essence of anything: why we were born, why we became sick, why we died. We could describe the processes and predict behavior based on previous observations, but the questions still remained.

I tried to remind myself that medicine had made progress over the years. There was anesthesia, so we didn't die of shock when parts of us were cut out. There were antibiotics so we didn't die of overwhelming bacterial infections. There were vaccines, so we could keep some viruses at bay. There was birth control so we could limit population growth and the dangers of childbirth. There were banked blood products, so we didn't suddenly bleed to death. But there were so many processes that we were hazy about.

So much about cancer was in the hazy territory that when we are told we have cancer, our whole life-story changes. I could sleep soundly the night before difficult cases in the Operating Room or between middle-of-the-night telephone calls from the Emergency Room, but when I had to tell someone they had cancer the next day, I hardly slept at all. I knew the impact of the news; you could see it in their faces. I tried to concentrate on a plan of action, but no one heard much after the word 'cancer' was used. And it was hard to be upbeat about chemotherapy and radiation when everyone had seen the side effects of the good cells being destroyed along with the bad. I rationalized that at least something could be done. I was certainly glad that radiation could be used for the tumor in Bertrand's brain.

I was already a physician when I first read Kafka's 'Metamorphosis', and I thought it was a heart-rending metaphor for sickness. You wake up one morning and find that embarrassing things are happening to your body which you can't control. You feel ashamed and hide yourself away as things progress, then you become unacceptable and unrecognizable to others in the end. I wanted to eradicate any shame that I could see in the eyes of those who were sick. Most of all, I wanted to disavow any sense of responsibility that they felt for their plight.

Bertrand was not self-conscious or ashamed of the speech impediment that he'd lived with all his life; so when he had no reservations about his illness, it was entirely predictable. He called many friends, young and old, whom he hadn't seen for years, arranged trips and picnics, and brought people together who would never have known each other otherwise. He confessed that his life felt unreal at times like he was playing a part in a movie, but he never succumbed to depression.

He was occasionally the victim of too much empathy in Telluride. I was at his house one day, and he asked, "Can you run to Sunshine Pharmacy and pick up my medications for me?" He looked fairly good, so it was unusual for him not to want to go outside.

"Sure, are you okay?"

"I'm fine, but I can't take any more hugs in the street."

"Okay, I promise not to hug you either."

"You can when you say Good-Bye."

37

BERTRAND WAS OBSESSED WITH THE IDEA of going to Mexico City, introducing us to the Creels, and traveling on to Patzcuaro to see the Purepechan people and clinic site, so we organized another trip a few months later. We included Jim Hanosh, my surgeon colleague, who was also excited to experience everything firsthand. I knew that we weren't going to be able to make much progress with the project from America and had braced myself, my office, and my patients for lots of quick trips.

We flew into Mexico City and had our meeting later that day. It was at an elegant restaurant called Casa Bel in the Polanco District. We sat at a sunny table outside, with our newly minted coffee-colored folders complete with Purepechan graphics and our name 'Operacion Michoacan', and waited for the Creels to arrive.

The air was so surprisingly perfect that the transition from inside to outside was imperceptible, Plates were going by with piles of succulent duck, roasted pulled pork, and glistening seafood. Our table was laden with the condiments to make the perfect bite; red chunky chipotle salsa, green tomatillo salsa draped in cilantro, fresh pico de gallo, and tiny soft corn tortillas. It was definitely more decadent than the Mexico I was used to.

The more time that we had to wait for them, the more I questioned the setting and who they really were. But when they arrived, they were the most unaffected, spontaneously charming people I had ever met. Their English was perfect, and they were interested in everything from Mexican and American politics to Wittgenstein. Luis Creel was an astute, thoughtful thirty year old who grew up solidly facing the conundrum of Mexico. Loli was in her twenties and had the grace of a gazelle; we were all mesmerized by her. She radiated sincerity and optimism.

We stayed for three hours, and the food was better than any John and I had sampled in all our trips to Mexico. It was novel to be in no hurry to do anything with the sound of the other tables enjoying themselves in the background. Luis and Loli left a little before we did, and we started to talk about how great it was that they were so enthusiastic about our ideas. Bertrand interjected, "Isn't there something so amazing about Latin women." John and Jim enthusiastically agreed, and they all launched into a discussion of what caused the added mystique. I felt like an gawky guy by comparison; notwithstanding their apologies when they remembered I was there.

When we got to Patzcuaro this time, the weather was sunny and warm. Both Bertrand and Jim were excited by how beautiful it was. We stayed in one of the oldest hotels from the eighteenth century whose windows had a series of heavy wooden shutters. When you opened them in the morning, the light streamed in from the plaza and was accompanied by the sound of sweeping and the smell of bread.

Jim and Bertrand hired Francisco for his proper purpose and came back beaming with masks and copper plates. Bertrand also befriended an older Purepechan woman on the plaza named Poncha. She sat demurely on a blanket under the portales and sold lace napkins. He would disappear to the other side of the street, and we would see him sitting on the ground beside her. They had long conversations in Spanish. When I met her, I was struck by her wizened face and the fact that she only came up to his waist when standing. She laughingly told me that he was planning to take her to Paris, and he bought napkins from her every day we were there.

Our meeting with the Creels fostered much optimism, but it was hard to predict how difficult it was going to be to accomplish something tangible. We met Willy, a combination realtor/architect/contractor, who showed us land and buildings. He had a sweet face, and his eyes welled up easily. Rather disturbingly, he never knew the price of anything or had any keys. Through another contact, we were introduced to Nancy, a nurse from America, who drove a truck loaded with medicines into the Purepechan mountain towns and ran clinics. She was in her fifties with a slight frame and bleached spiked hair. She was tough, committed, and the only source of medical care in many of their communities. Luis and Loli set up a meeting for us with the Secretary of Health in the state capitol, Morelia. We nervously waited in a government building and met with Maria Austria, an elegant doctor in her thirties, who seemed very supportive and showed us lists of existing medical facilities and reviewed the most pressing needs.

In between all those encounters, we explored beautiful streets, marveled at colonial architecture, found murals in government buildings, ate mole and traditional stews, and drank beer and margaritas. Towards the end of our stay, we met Willy's father, a local doctor, who felt it crucial that we meet with the Patzcuaro physicians to let them know what we were doing. By chance, the local medical community had a meeting scheduled, but it was the night before our flight from Mexico City which left at eight o'clock in the morning.

We worried about Bertrand, but he wouldn't hear of us postponing a presentation of our project because of his health. He thought it was important for the physicians from the two countries to work together from the inception. Our proposal was presented by Willy, with Jim and I standing beside him, and was surprisingly well-received. We sleepily started our four hour drive from Patzcuaro to Mexico City at eleven thirty that night. In a typical John fashion, we had no maps or any idea where the airport was. At four in the morning, when we arrived in God-knows-what part of Mexico City, we got directions from the drunks and the prostitutes. We arrived at the airport as easily as if it had been England in broad daylight.

38

ABOUT A MONTH AFTER WE GOT BACK, I lost my second dog. We had to take Beth to the Vet's office to be put down because she couldn't stand up anymore. She was so deaf that for the last year I could communicate with her only by clapping; I'll always remember her happy look of recognition when she heard my hands behind her. When we picked her up on the reservation, starving at six months old, she looked like a fruit bat because she was one of those shepherd crosses with such big ears. Of all my dogs, she was the most eager to please. She never seemed to forget how much she loved us and how much she wanted to be good so she could stay. We put her in the cave with Sam on an early spring day when the desert was bursting with purple flowers. John said he was only bones by then.

Everything on the farm went well that summer. There were plenty of grape clusters hanging on the vines, and we miraculously avoided any rain for the first two cuts of hay, so the barn was full. I liked to climb to the top of the stacked bales and sit and smell the new hay; it reminded me of green beans.

Bertrand wasn't able to work in his restaurant anymore, so he moved to their ranch nearby. Anyone else would have used the opportunity to slow down, but he did the opposite. His attitude about further treatment had become half-hearted, so he had plenty of time to travel. It was clear that he knew his time was limited; he insisted on so many group photographs in Mexico that it broke my heart.

I worked hard to make ends meet with my practice and was nervous about every fluctuation in my surgery schedule. John became obsessed with selling the wine and was out more nights than he was in. My surgeries increased in Monticello, so I was there for at least four days a month. I explored Canyonlands and Blue Mountain in my free time during the day, but at night it felt like a prison; especially when John called from a raucous dinner in Dunton or a busy restaurant in Durango.

Discussing the project seemed to take up much of the time that John and I spent together. He was anxious to be in control, and it was difficult for me to acknowledge his authority because, for once, I felt more qualified. I steeled myself daily, so I couldn't be bullied, and carefully chose the mountains I would die defending.

I remember one argument we had in front of Pancho at teatime. All of us were sweating from drinking hot tea in the kitchen when it was ninety degrees outside. The last thing we needed was a heated conversation.

"How's it going with the doctors? Do you have some who want to volunteer in Mexico?" John nodded towards Pancho.

"Yeah, everyone does. They all get pretty excited when I tell them about it." Pancho was grinning from ear to ear.

"We need letters of commitment from all of them."

"What?" This was totally out of the blue.

"I want them to sign a form promising to commit two weeks every year."

"I think it's a bit premature."

"We can't go on unless we have proof in numbers. How hard can it be to get them to sign something?" Pancho looked concerned, and I wondered if he thought John was making sense because I certainly didn't.

"I've got verbal commitments. Why do they need to sign something? We don't even have a place for them to work yet."

"I guess you doctors are too God-like to actually have to commit on paper." John's tone of voice was worsening, and Pancho was now frowning.

"I just think it's unnecessary." I didn't add that I also thought it was going to be embarrassing and stupid.

"I think it's crucial. Come on Pancho, let's get back to work."

John left later that evening to sell wine in Telluride and spend the night with Bertrand. I slept outside on the porch in a bed I had made for the summer covered in lacy pillows and surrounded by a white mosquito net. In the morning, I woke up early and made new lists.

What we've done so far:
   We've put together promotional folders.
   We have verbal commitments from specialists and surgeons in the
      U.S.
   We have funding from Katrin and Christoph to start the project.
   We've met the Creels and have a government connection.
   Willy wants to be our contractor, and he seems committed and
      honest.
   Nancy, the American nurse, wants to work with us.
   We've received approval from the Secretary of Health in Morelia.
   We have verbal support from the local physicians in Patzcuaro.

The next steps:
   We need to decide what health care we will be able to provide.
   We need to work with Nancy to become familiar with the
      population.
   We need to decide where to place the project; in or out of town.
   We have to either buy land or an existing building and work out the
      details.
   We need to get equipment donated from hospitals in the U.S.
   We have to figure out how to move things across the border.
   We need to become a tax free entity in the U.S.
   We need to plan fundraising for the future.
   We have to put together a Board and have meetings.
   We need protocols, formularies, and job descriptions.

What seems impossible right now:
   Speaking Spanish well enough to function.
   Trying to estimate how much it will all cost.
   Getting more people to donate money.
   Putting together a hospital from scratch in a foreign country.

39

THE SUN WAS GETTING LOWER, and I had walked too far. Jessie followed directly behind me like she did when she was exhausted; I had to be careful not to lift my back foot too high or I would hit her chin. I chose Jessie, the black Lab-cross, because her stamina was amazing, and she was too nervous to wander far. She was the least intelligent of the bunch, and I was drawn to her because she needed me more than the others. In her eyes, the world was a confusing, frightening place, and I was the one she looked to for help. When we moved to the farm, it took her four months to notice Gene's cows in the alfalfa field next to their kennel. She barked at them for days afterwards with an alarmed look; I always wondered what it was that finally caught her attention.

I had never ventured as deep into Ute territory, but I had also not reached the place I was looking for. I knew there had to be a pool at the top of Rock Creek where all the Cottonwoods were clustered, Gene said he remembered going there as a boy, but I was nowhere near high enough.

We had covered some rough ground following deer trails. I would have been totally lost had I not been careful to stay within eyeshot of the dry creek bed. It was hard to imagine how much further the pool could be. I'd been out for four hours, which meant four to get back. I decided that next time I would leave at the crack of dawn in the summer, so there would be at least fourteen hours of light. I also decided to have no dogs along because they were all so willing that it made me feel guilty. I knew they could head back to the house at any time, but I also knew they would never leave me alone on a mountainside.

The terrain got a little greener on the Ute Mountain as you got higher, but you had to look hard to notice. It was mostly tumbled boulders, twisted stumps of pinion and juniper, and a few towering cedars. The creek bed was so full of fallen leaves and branches that it was difficult to picture the running water in the spring. I was listening so intently that I heard every bird that hopped off a branch. A woman was attacked by a mountain lion on the other side of the mountain a few years ago, but it was a toothless female who couldn't hunt for anything better to eat.

I thought I would have no appetite, but I had gulped down the whole of my tupperware container of mixed peanuts and raisins. I was out of water because I had wasted quite a bit by pouring it into hollows in the rock for Jessie. She always lapped more away than she drank; I jealously watched it running down the hill.

I turned for home defeated and started to cry. I knew the tears were going to surface again sooner or later. I couldn't believe he was gone. Bertrand could have gotten me to the place that I wanted to go. I probably expected that his ghost would be there to help me, but all I could feel was his absence.

The ground was so tortured and covered in bleached bones. There was evidence of death around every corner; little chiseled prairie dog skulls, dried out deer legs with golden fur and delicate black hooves, calf pelvises with femurs still attached by hardened sinews. I fingered the piece of china in my pocket; my treasure from the excursion. I found it on a cliff above the part of the creek that I thought was the most terrifying. During a flash flood long ago, the roaring water filled the whole valley, and it brought much of the mountain down with it. When it receded, there remained the most graphic evidence of destruction. There were enormous uprooted trees lying at all angles with huge boulders wedged underneath and against them. It was impassable on foot, and nothing had changed since the water had done its work.

The china was a piece of a bone-colored plate with two faded pink flowers on the front and the words 'Tudor Rose' on the back. I was quite sure that it meant that a woman had once lived close-by, and I despaired when I thought of her life in that harsh valley, below the barren mountain, hundreds of miles from anywhere.

It was after dark when I finally made it home. John was out selling wine and Pancho was away for the weekend, so no one was worried. Jessie was starving and so were the other dogs; the poor things had been locked in their cages for hours. They howled in unison when I left and barked for joy on my return.

As I stacked their four full dinner bowls, I remembered how much it amused Bertrand to see me emerging from the house balancing six of them. I felt him with me again and knew I would never really lose him. He would still be there with me when I was traveling, reading, cooking, listening to music, eating picnics, and climbing mountains. I just had to pay attention.

Bertrand enjoyed every good moment that life gave him. He even managed to bring friends down to the farm for the vintage a few weeks before he died. After dinner on the night of the last harvest, I could feel him gazing at me from across the room as I moved around the kitchen. I smiled and tried to catch his eye, but his concentration was fixed both on me and somewhere deep inside himself.

He was cared for by a team of wonderful hospice nurses who all loved him, and he died quietly at home. The last words he uttered before slipping into a coma seemed to be in preparation for a picnic at the beach. He wanted Noelle, his wife, to make a list for him: hats, flip-flops, towels, and, of course, lots of food.

40

JOHN AND I FINALLY ARRANGED TO HAVE A DINNER out together at the Kennebeck Cafe near Durango in late November. I badly needed cheering up and had spent most of the month after Bertrand's death in the upstairs bedroom. It was a beautiful starry night, and the mountains were already in deep snow. I was still tearful, but eager to get out for a glass of wine and more decadent dinner. Our friend Barbara, the owner, gave us a table by the window. The snow sparkled from the reflected light, and the restaurant felt cozy and warm in juxtaposition. There was a small vase of pale pink roses with countless petals on the table, and the kitchen emanated smells of grilled meat and roasted garlic.

After we ordered our food, John got up and engaged a table or two to talk about our wine; the Kennebeck was one of our best promoters and sold many bottles on a nightly basis. The interest in the restaurant grew, our food came, and he never returned to sit down with me. I ate alone and tried to appreciate how hard he worked at marketing, but I decided that it would be my last dinner out with him for a while. I knew better than to talk to him about it because he would be self-righteous.

True to his word, John had little or no reaction to Bertrand's death. I concluded that this meant he was either supremely enlightened or frighteningly shallow. When I asked him how he felt, he owned up to the latter and said death simply didn't bother him. This was even more puzzling because Bertrand was the only friend we had who was John's age; all the rest were closer to mine. I couldn't imagine that he felt nothing. At the very least, I anticipated that he would reflect on his own mortality.

I was a mess. My emotions were entirely out of the control of my intellect, and there was nothing to do but weather the storm. John said I was being selfish and it was true; I was only grieving for myself. But I was so sad to think I would never see Bertrand or hear his voice again. He was so ravaged by the end that I worried that my memories of him would be as I last saw him, but they weren't. In no time, he was back to normal in my mind's eye.

Practicing medicine delayed my acceptance of death as a natural process. We were always fighting for life at all costs, so death signified a failure. To some degree, there was a denial that it was ever supposed to occur; so for a long time, when someone died, I tried to figure out how the medical profession had let them down. In the course of my career, I realized the fallaciousness of assigning blame for something that was going to eventually happen to everyone. I also rejected the Doctor-as-God complex that initiated this line of thinking in the first place. I still felt I had a long way to go before I could accept death with equanimity; but if John was any example, I wasn't sure that I wanted to.

Medicine also failed to bring me any closer to understanding death. I knew more than I wanted to know about birth, and the more it was explained, the less miraculous it seemed. With death, I knew the science of how it happened and why it happened, but it seemed to amount to nothing. By not knowing what happened after death, I didn't know anything at all. Heraclitus said, *All men are equally mystified by unaccountable evidence, even Homer, wisest of the Greeks. He was mystified by children catching lice. He heard them say, what we have found and caught we throw away; what we have not found and caught we still have.* I had thrown away the beginning of life, and the end was still a mystery.

The Navajo were the first truly fatalistic culture I had known. Sometimes their passivity was disconcerting. One day in Shiprock, I heard that the brother of my clinic nurse was found beaten to death underneath a car. The supervisor who told me the story said, "What we usually do when this happens is collect a fund." I was taken aback that violence of this magnitude would be spoken of and dealt with as a matter of fact. The underlying notion that things like this were unavoidable was very disturbing.

Most of the time, though, the peace that their acceptance of fate gave them was like a drug to me. I was soothed by their conversation, and it didn't seem to matter whether it was in English or Navajo (that I still couldn't understand). I decided that it would be therapeutic for me to take care of the hay calls during December. When the trucks full of Navajos drove up to the hay barn and blasted their horns, I ran out and sold it to them just so I could hear them laughing and talking in that slow cadence that seemed so calm and timeless.

41

WE WERE CONFIDENT ENOUGH after our last visit to Mexico to earnestly search for a physical place to put the clinic. In the early part of 2004, I took my family to Patzcuaro with that in mind. Willy, the Mexican realtor and architect, had no email address, so Pancho helped me with a phone call to let him know we were on our way.

Callie and my parents were coming from Charlotte, and we were all to meet in Houston for the connecting flight to Mexico. I was in the airport frantically looking for them when Callie called to say that they were going to be a day late arriving because Daddy had forgotten the passports. I was astounded. It seemed so unlike him.

She was unwilling to offer more details, so I told her that I would buy a phone card and call her from Mexico the next morning to arrange a driver. My parents had travelled abroad so many times that I couldn't imagine them not having their passports with them. And my father was the most organized person on earth; everything that he owned was neatly filed away in stacks of carefully labeled boxes.

When I got in touch with Callie the next day, my parents were upstairs and she was on her own downstairs crying. She said that she had noticed that Daddy was forgetful at Christmas, but was shocked this time at the progression of his confusion. I had last seen him over the summer; and he seemed quieter than usual, but otherwise normal.

When I thought about it more, I realized that he was always the one who used to call to find out about what was going on in my life. For the past six months, it had been my mother calling; he was quickly on and off the phone. I had been so inattentive that I hadn't even missed him. I hadn't even realized he was going away.

I was apprehensive about the trip; but when they arrived, he was happy to be in Mexico; it had always been one of his favorite places. We stayed at the old hotel on the plaza. Daddy kept either forgetting or ignoring the rules and smoking in the room.

I found Willy, and we looked at some land that might be available and the outside of more buildings that we didn't have keys for. I was beginning to have my doubts about Willy, so I asked around and discovered another realtor, Hector, who operated out of a shoe shop. Within a day, we had looked inside a couple of good buildings and at a large tract of land on the outskirts of town. I told Willy that we would be working with both of them for the time being, and he still had us to his house for a traditional breakfast of bread and chocolate before we left.

I had been counting on help in Mexico from my father who was full of common sense and had given me good practical advice over the years, but it was too late. I realized that I would have to develop more confidence in my own opinions from then on.

We went to see the sights in Morelia and ate roast chicken with our fingers on a bench in the park. I was surprised to see my mother function quite well without silverware. I found Poncha still sitting on her blanket on the plaza in Patzcuaro and didn't have the Spanish or the heart to tell her Bertrand had died. I gave her twenty dollars. She tried to give me napkins in exchange; but I smiled, shook my head no, and walked away.

We watched Daddy closely in the Houston airport, but managed to lose him anyway. He went into the bathroom with the three of us standing outside the door and didn't reappear. After waiting for fifteen minutes, we asked a man, who was going in, to call out his name; and he immediately returned with him. We asked no questions. His dementia was not a mild case, but my mother seemed to be handling him fairly well. He certainly enjoyed himself on the trip. On the way back, it made me smile to overhear him, in the front of the plane, complimenting me to my mother, but I heard no reply from her end.

Spring came to the canyon, and it still didn't lift my spirits. The Meadowlark's solitary notes could be heard during the day, and we lit smudge pots under the fruit trees to protect them from the cold at night. It looked like a fairyland from the bedroom window upstairs with all the tiny flames tenuous and hopeful down below.

My residency in Obstetrics had turned me into a master of compartmentalizing, so I was the only one who knew I was sad. We were taught early that it was crucial in Medicine to function no matter what was bothering you; be it lack of food, lack of sleep, other sick patients, a problem with a colleague, the fact that there was no life left at home to have a problem with. The other great skill we learned was not to acknowledge we were human and needed to do the things that other people did. One of the angriest patients, I remember seeing during my internship, was upset because when I came to see her I had pillow marks on my cheek in the middle of the day. We furtively ate, slipped away to the bathroom, stayed awake for days, and worked no matter how sick we felt.

I was still flogging away at my projects on the farm, but after three years, they felt empty and repetitive. I used the Solarflex machine to relieve tension like a Gerbil on a wheel. Jessie was the only dog who would come with me up the Battlerock, and she came without much enthusiasm. Pancho and I had both given up speaking any Spanish to each other beyond 'Good Morning. Have a nice day.' And the piano pieces I wanted to play were too challenging. I kept reminding myself that spring was on its way, but, for the first time in my life, I could feel my patience running out.

42

BERTRAND WANTED HIS ASHES TO BE CAST from the top of his favorite mountain, Lone Cone, and we all waited for the snow-melt to do it. It was a hot day in July, and we were snaking up the road in our cars. I had been feeling okay when we started, but now I was weak and dizzy. I was worried that at any minute I might drive off the narrow dirt road and careen down the mountain; there was a sheer drop to my left that seemed oddly enticing. I tried to remember which car John hopped into when we started. Why was I in the car by myself?

I found a place to pull off, then signaled to the car behind me to stop. I was so relieved to get in the car with somebody else that I didn't even notice where I was leaving mine. There were two European women in this one, which made me feel even more incompetent. The driver was Marie, who I had met some years ago with Bertrand, and the other I had never seen before. We arrived at the bottom of the trail, and about thirty of us got out of the cars and looked around. The mountaintop was one huge scree field that stretched for miles with unsteady boulders as big as cement blocks.

Noelle gave the heavy sack of ashes to Olivier, a young French athlete, to carry up the uneven rocks. The mountain looked challenging; I had only been up the smaller version to the right of it. I surveyed the group and noticed that some of the people, who wanted to be here to say good-bye, had no business tackling this climb.

It took forever, but everyone helped each other and we made it to the summit. The mountain stood alone, hence the name. The ground stretched out from all sides below in a patchwork of green and brown. The sun was shining and the sky was cloudless, but it was still windy and cold on the top.

I sat off to one side with Julian, Noelle and Bertrand's son, trying not to cry. Olivier made cairns of stone, Marie secured the prayer flags, and Noelle asked John to say a few words. "Bertrand told me what to do when he was alive, and he's still ordering me around when he's dead." No one laughed. I silently promised Bertrand that, come hell or high water, I would succeed with the clinic in Mexico.

Noelle opened the plastic bag of ashes, and I felt an instant of revulsion when she brought it over for me to get a handful. They were heavy and greasy, and I could feel bits of bone in them. I threw them off the side, said a prayer for him, and watched the string of prayer flags fluttering to endlessly repeat it.

It took even longer to get people back down the mountain, but the afternoon clouds held off as if they understood. Olivier went up three times to support the ones who were most unsteady. The grass in the meadow at the bottom was particularly soft and inviting after the endless rock. We spread a huge tablecloth and unpacked fois gras, smoked salmon, crusty bread, aioli, and mounds of cheese and fruit just like he would have wanted us to.

We toasted him with numerous glasses of wine and cognac and celebrated his life; some with words, some with silence. When we left, we hugged each other good-bye realizing, that without him around to bring us together, some of us would never see each other again. John and I drove the two hours home in his car and left mine on the mountainside. He was still cross because he thought I was being overly emotional.

"How could you still be this upset. Were you having an affair with Bertrand?" I thought that he surely didn't mean what he said.

"How could you ask me that question? Of course not. I'm behaving like a normal human being. You're the one who's the freak."

"Don't you think you've milked it for all it's worth?"

"I haven't said a word about it to you in months."

"So what happened today?"

"It was his funeral."

"At some point you're going to have to get over it."

"I'll get over it when I'm over it. At some point you're going to have to face up to it. "

"I have faced up to it."

"Don't you miss him?"

"I'm too busy right now to miss anybody."

"Me included."

"I'm out all the time because I need to sell the wine. In fact, I want to convert the bottom floor of the tower into a tasting room and put signs on the road this fall." I hadn't heard this idea before.

"It's my home. I can't have strangers on my porches drinking wine all day. There's nowhere for me to get away if I'm on call."

"We need to be commercial, or it will never make a profit. We've spent a small fortune already. This isn't a hobby anymore."

"There must be some other alternative."

"None that doesn't involve money for another building to put it in."

He had me between a rock and a hard place. Speaking of which, a week later, it took us all day driving around Lone Cone to finally find my car.

43

THE HARVEST IN 2004 WAS ABOUT THE SAME as the year before. We made a Chardonnay that year, but the red grape numbers were down because our vineyard was affected by late frost and there was not much production from the vines near Pancho's house yet.

John did make the bottom floor of the tower into a tasting room of sorts and started having lunches and dinners for local restaurant staff. I hid in my bedroom in the back of the house and tried to escape the eye of the visitors on the porch when I snuck into the kitchen to grab a snack.

The first really cold weekend in the fall, I was by myself on the farm because John had gone to Grand Junction where most of the other Colorado wines were made. I couldn't go very far because of call, so I read most of the day by the fire. I ran into Pancho in the late afternoon when I went out to get more wood. We tasted the newly bottled 2003 Merlot in the wine house; and he asked me to his house for dinner, but I declined because I was worried about being a too-frequent guest.

I fed the dogs, put them in their cages, and let Laura, the Rottweiller, into the mud-room for protection since there were no working locks on the doors. I felt so lonely. John hadn't even put his arm around me since Bertrand died. He was out almost every night, he was drinking a ton, and when he was home he was on the computer in the guest house until long after I had gone to sleep. I still left him a cup of tea on the bedside table before I went to work, but there was no hope that he would be awake before I left the house anymore.

I drilled him about what was wrong. I showed him a list of the symptoms of a Major Depressive Disorder to prove to him that he was depressed, but he considered himself above the common ailments, especially the mental ones. Pancho and I spun around him like tops to do everything that needed to be done. We had both given up on him snapping out of it any time soon.

He was so different from the person that I once knew; he was angry, argumentative, and bitter. His sense of humor had gone missing, and the only times I saw him smiling or laughing were when he was plied with alcohol. The whole world seemed to annoy him instead of amusing him as it had before. And nothing escaped his criticism.

I couldn't fathom how he could be bitter with everything we had. When I questioned him, he claimed that he thought he would have accomplished something big by this point in his life; much bigger than owning a vineyard and making wine. Everyone had expected great things from him, and now he hadn't the time left to do anything great. I decided that one of the few benefits of being a woman was that no one expected much from you, so everything you did was a bonus.

When I thought about what the 'great thing' was that he hadn't done, I supposed he meant writing a book. He had always wanted to write. When we moved in together, he came with boxes of loosely bound manuscript. In my limited, twenty-five year old opinion, his writing had promise. My goal was to give him the opportunity to flourish, the time to think, and the space to be creative. So when I finished residency, we set up house based on the premise that I would work doing medicine, which was what I loved to do, and he would be creative.

The way I saw it, over the years, he had two basic problems that kept him from writing the book he'd always wanted to write. The first was his vanity; creating the dramatic backdrop that he felt he needed to be creative was more important than the act itself. The second was his lack of discipline; there were interesting diversions around every corner. Out of our combined character strengths and flaws, the farm was born, grew and developed. I fought it at first, then fell in love with it. John loved and hated it from the beginning.

I had no idea what I'd done to deserve his increasing negligence. I was close to paying off the farm and vineyard from efficiently running my practice. I had excelled at cooking, canning, gardening, animal husbandry, butchering, doing dishes and laundry, cleaning, reading, music, and hiking. It was hard to believe this was where we were after twenty years of marriage. When people congratulated me in the past for being married so long and said it must have been hard work at times, I denied that it was any work at all. Now it was tons of work, and I wasn't getting anywhere. I simply didn't know how to reach him.

I slowly began to accept the fact that I wasn't able to make John happy anymore. And since I hadn't succeeded, I resented all the years I had wasted with him as my main focus. I wondered how the magic of our lives could fall short for him; it was more than I could have ever dreamt of: a beautiful farm and vineyard in a rugged landscape, two imaginative, colorful houses, an eclectic collection of books, rugs, and paintings, sixty acres of lovely green alfalfa, ten acres of trellised vines, all the unfenced land you could possibly use for hiking and riding on either side, water for irrigation, fertile soil for growing, horses, dogs, barns, hay sheds, corrals, chickens, air so clear that the stars were overwhelming, a place so safe we'd never had keys to the house, a simple medical practice doing meaningful work for a grateful population, an authentic western town with sheep tied in the back of pick-ups in the grocery store parking lot.

Camus once said, *Ah, mon cher, for anyone who is alone, without God and without a master, the weight of days is dreadful. Hence one must choose a master, God being out of style.* John was my master; I worshiped him. What did you do when your master went bonkers, when he didn't want to own you anymore? Why had we changed from being the perfect couple into being a disaster?

The fire had gone out, and I was cold and ready for my first night of the season sleeping in soft flannel sheets. I stopped by the mud-room to lie down with Laura on her blanket and hug her goodnight before I went to bed.

44

AFTER CHRISTMAS, WE HEADED BACK TO MEXICO. Since they were funding the clinic start-up, Katrin and Christoph wanted to see the prospective sites; and I wanted to investigate what care was actually available, so we could decide what was most needed. Eight of us went, Flying Doctors of Mercy style, in Christoph's Lear jet. I expected glamour and got what seemed more like a trip in the family station wagon. We drove up to the airplane, hauled out our suitcases, piled them in the bathroom because there was no room anywhere else, and had cheese nabs and Budweisers out of a vinyl cooler. The party consisted of us, Bella, David, Katrin, Christoph, and 2 other friends: Annabelle and Drew, who spoke flawless Castilian Spanish.

We spent the first night in Morelia, the state capital, and suffered a mariachi serenade from two to four a.m. in front of a neighboring hotel on the plaza. Since I couldn't arrange an appointment beforehand at the Civil Hospital, which was the referral center for the poor in Patzcuaro, I decided to take Drew with me and simply look around.

We were bleary-eyed the next day when the taxi pulled up to a cement building thronged with medical staff and sick people. I was immediately self-conscious because I was wearing a spaghetti strap top and a sheer sweater. I felt a bit skimpily dressed to be in a hospital, but I expected to ask a few questions and be dismissed so I told myself not to worry. Drew spoke to a doctor, and, either owing to my attire or his beautiful Spanish, the two of us were whisked upstairs to the office of the Neurosurgeon who ran the hospital. He was charming and very excited about our ideas. He called physicians and arranged tours of all the various departments. In Surgery, they asked if I wanted to help with the case load that day. I pulled my sweater a bit more together in the front, smiled, and assumed they were kidding.

The hospital was so primitive by American standards that I worked hard to cover up my grimaces with smiles as we rounded every corner. The area for laboring women consisted of eight beds pushed very close together with no curtains between them. The delivery room down the hall could be shared by four women. It had a big drain in the center, threatening metal tables, and individual plastic buckets to catch the blood. The patients stood in endless lines for the clinics downstairs; we were told they came and slept in the park across the street for days before they got to the front. The doctors worked hard and were proud of their facility, but the number of patients was overwhelming.

In Patzcuaro, we were able to reconnect with Nancy, the American nurse with the portable pharmacy in her pick-up. She took us to a Purepechan village where the women gathered near an elementary school, and we all drank Nescafe huddled in kindergarten chairs around an impossibly low table. She said that there had originally been clinics in all the villages, but most of them, in the remote areas, had either stopped functioning or had no medicines. The indigenous women were pleasant and quiet, but it was evident that they had heard many promises in the past and would believe it when they saw it.

We looked at more land and buildings with Hector and Willy and enlisted a Century 21 branch in Mexico as well. I found Poncha and gave her another twenty dollars.

A month later, we found the perfect building for the clinic. It was a six classroom school house which had never functioned due to problems with permits. The structure seemed sound, it was on the outskirts of town, and it already looked like a clinic from the outside. We walked around one of the gigantic identical rooms, that Willy actually had a key to open, and bought it without seeing the others. Katrin and Christoph wired the money, and John planned another trip to get the paperwork in order.

On the way back, we met a friend of Loli Creel's named Paulina. She was a lawyer in Mexico City, and her father was the current Financial

Minister of Mexico. She was stunningly beautiful with black hair and clear blue eyes. She was also very astute. She offered to work on our legal status in Mexico through her firm which was the most prominent one in the city. We had dinner with Luis, Loli, Paulina, and assorted others in a Spanish restaurant with hanging hams and olives. It lasted past midnight, but no one really noticed.

I couldn't wait to update my lists when I got back:

What we've done so far:
    We've purchased the perfect building for the clinic.
    We've enlisted Paulina to work on our legal structure in Mexico.
    I've received donations of supplies and equipment from America.
    We've put together a loose Board who has seen the target population.
    We have Nancy's support which will help with getting the people's
        trust.
    We've visited the referral hospital in Morelia, and they're receptive.

The next steps:
    We need to decide whether we want an inpatient hospital or a clinic.
    Then we need to draw up basic architectural plans with Willy.
    We need to stay in touch with Luis, Loli, and Paulina.
    We need Nancy's data to know what diseases are out there.
    We have to start figuring out how to cross the border with the
        donations.
    We need to start the legal work in the U.S., so we can begin raising
        funds.

What seems impossible right now:
Putting it all together to form a medical facility

45

MY NEPHEWS HAD BEEN COMING to see us in Colorado ever since they were eight and ten years old. I had watched them change from children who needed official airline escorts between flights to big, tall teenagers who wanted to go rock climbing. We spent the summers with them camping, hiking, climbing, kayaking; and John got them up early to do chores around the farm and work in the vineyard.

I made a plan in the summer of 2005 for Miles and McKinnon to come with Callie to Dunton. Callie was one of the most prominent Southern caterers and the Dunton Hot Springs resort was magical in the summer, so I decided to bring the two together. I knew that Callie and the boys would love Dunton, and I wanted David, Bella, Katrin, and Christoph to get a taste of authentic Southern food.

They were going to stay for a week and spend the first three days in Dunton, the following two camping, and then the last couple of days on the farm. There were going to be two big Southern dinners in Dunton, and the boys were helping Callie with both the cooking and serving the food. John, meanwhile, planned a trip to the Northeast that coincided with their visit. He had an idea for a book about the sixties from a woman's point of view and wanted to interview an old girlfriend in Vermont. He was going to be away for their arrival and the first dinner, but then had a flight to return on the second night with all of us in Dunton.

On the third day, we were all going to embark on an overnight camping trip in Utah with two days of hiking around Canyonlands. I had discovered some new trails during one of my stays in Monticello and found a perfect place to pitch some tents. The Dunton crowd loved camping in the desert, and, with Callie along, we could do it with delicious food. I had even taken a couple of days off work.

The old saloon in Dunton had a bar that boasted carvings from Butch Cassidy and the Sundance kid. It was overflowing with glasses of wildflowers, and I was sitting at the bar by myself sipping Dickel Tennessee whisky. The sun had gone down behind the hills, but there was still plenty of light outside. There was going to be a full moon up later, and Callie's food smelled great, but my enthusiasm was gone. I just wanted to get it over with.

John was supposed to be flying in from Vermont, but he called Dunton and left a message with the staff to say that he was going to be a week delayed. That meant he wouldn't see my nephews, and a big part of the reason they came out West was to see John. They loved John, and it had been two years since they'd last seen him because both of them couldn't come the summer before. Now God only knew when they would see him again.

I asked the manager if John explained what had happened or left a number where I could call him back. She said apologetically that he was going to try to call me tomorrow because his cellphone wasn't working well. He also left a message with Bella, and when I complained to her about him not calling me directly, she said it was because he knew I was busy with Callie and the boys.

Katrin, Christoph, Bella, and David got so excited about the food that it ended up being contagious. There was a full Southern menu of roasted corn soup, smothered quail, and fried okra. I added a little more of the Sutcliffe Merlot than I should have to the Dickel.

I was staying in the ghost town, so I wandered down to my cabin for the night which was ironically called 'Honeymoon'. It had a red and black hundred year old Navajo rug on the wall, a quilt on the bed made of patchwork hides, and lots of pictures of cowboys. I fell asleep with the gentle sound of the West Fork of the Dolores River running beside my room and woke up with a headache in the morning.

We called off the Utah camping trip and decided to go down to Canyonlands for the day instead with a picnic of egg salad sandwiches and chocolate chip cookies. Callie wanted to stay in Dunton to rest; so Katrin, Bella, my nephews, and I headed out to explore one of my trails. It was a mercifully cool day for July. We were enticed by dark caves across deep gullies and were thwarted on our paths by unexpected cliffs and drops only ropes would resolve. Throughout the day, I had the odd feeling that Katrin and Bella were trying a little too hard to keep me cheerful.

Callie and the boys spent two extra nights in Dunton and their last night with me in McElmo on the farm. We stopped at Citimarket on the way home to pick up some groceries and a video. When we got to the house, I checked that my cellphone was working for the hundredth time that day and was sad to find no messages from John on the answering machine. I knew better than to try to call him; he had always called me. Ever since the early days, when he was out dancing in Charleston during my residency, I didn't want to waste the time or the energy worrying about what he was up to. I could be practical then, but it didn't seem to be working now; I simply wasn't able to put it out of my mind.

We made a simple supper, then Callie and I had an earnest discussion about the state of my marriage in the kitchen while the boys joked with Pancho on the porch. We went to the guest house afterwards to watch the video on the second floor of the tower, where our only TV sat in front of a two story window. I tried to stay interested, but found myself really watching the dying light, the creek at the bottom of the vines, and the mountainside behind wondering what in the hell I was going to do.

It felt futile to have a conversation with John, because he couldn't really listen, and he talked round and round a subject until you came out feeling dazed and confused. We'd never had serious fights or problems that required earnest discussion during our twenty year relationship, so we had no way of dealing with things when they weren't perfect. And he absolutely refused to go to therapy when I suggested it.

It was hard to believe that he didn't love the boys enough to want to come home and see them. He blatantly said that he never wanted to see my parents again because he had so many problems with my mother over the years. But it was also strange to me that he didn't love my father enough to want to see him either. Even with Daddy's dementia and our abbreviated phone conversations, he always asked about John and said to tell him 'hello'. I could only hope he was demented enough not to realize that John didn't care. John didn't seem to care about anything but himself right now, me included.

I was embarrassed, and I was angry. My father told John, when he met him, that he had never seen me lose my temper, even as a child. I discovered that I had a temper after all and was so close to being out of control that I found it frightening.

46

I LEFT HIM BEFORE HE GOT BACK and went to stay at the Holiday Inn in town. When he called, there was no discussion, I simply suggested he find somewhere to live. The next day, I was back at the farm and he was at Jim Hanosh's, our friend the surgeon. It was exhilarating at first, but it wore off quickly.

I tried as hard as I could to stay clear and decisive. I tried to ignore his incredulity and distress. I tried to cut off his voice in my head every minute of every day. I tried to be heartless about the obvious depression that he wouldn't admit to. I tried not to listen to Pancho when he said how sad John was.

Pancho kept saying that he wanted the 'old John' back. I did too, but I didn't know where the 'old John' was. John had all but stopped the work that made him happy on the farm. At sixty two, he was hanging around with twenty and thirty year olds, getting in brawls at bars after wine-tastings, driving home drunk and wrecking cars. He was critical of everyone. There were days when Pancho could do nothing right. Navajo friends came to buy hay and he complained about how lazy they were. He even yelled at a six year old child for running into the field and potentially damaging the hay.

In the meantime, I concentrated on my work and the chores on the farm. Doing surgery had always stripped away the world outside; I thought of the Operating Room as a parallel reality. I was happy to do more operations because they took my mind off everything else. Every patient's procedure and recovery was an evolving story that I followed with interest, and those stories could make me forget about my own for a moment.

Home was another matter; almost everything was painful. I moved to the upstairs bedroom and struggled to keep eating and sleeping. The house seemed so empty without him. Fortunately, Pancho was there to help keep the farm in order.

August was stiflingly hot, and I had another sick dog. Dusty, the Border Collie cross, was the smartest dog I ever had the pleasure of owning; she not only understood English, but the spelling I did to elude her. Once, when she was only a six-week old puppy, she jumped in and tried to swim across a roaring creek to follow John to the other side. She was currently the oldest one, and I had been pureeing her food in a blender for quite some time because she couldn't swallow solids anymore.

I had maintained my resolve to stay separated from John for a month when she started coughing up even the blended food. After a week, I knew that I needed to decide whether to take her in to be put to sleep, and she was John's dog too and John's favorite dog at that. I needed his opinion, but I also needed his help. I just couldn't bring myself to take her to the vet, so I decided to call John and see what he wanted to do.

"Hi John, it's me."

"Emily, it's so good to hear your voice. I'm trying to leave the farm every day by the time you get home from work, but it's hard because I want to see you."

"I don't have good news. Dusty is really sick. She's been vomiting up even the blended food for more than a week."

"I knew it couldn't be long. Her eyes look dull, and she's so skinny."

"I think she should be put to sleep, but I can't bring myself to take her in."

"I'll take care of it. I've taken care of all the other animals for you. Don't worry, I know it's hard for you."

"It's hard for you too."

"Everything is hard for me right now. I miss you so much, Emily. Don't even think about it twice. I'll take her in tomorrow and put her in the cave with the others when it's over."

"I'm so sorry."

"It's sad, but it's got to be done."

John moved back to the farm after Dusty died. I decided I would rather continue with things as they were than endure any more sadness. I also couldn't desert John when he needed me the most. I had to find a way to deal with his mid-life crisis, depression, or whatever it was. I knew that the man I married was in there somewhere, was miserable, and needed my help. And I was sure I could make him happy again if I tried hard enough. Besides, if I constantly had a running commentary from him in my head, I might as well have him in person.

We were both relieved and excited to be together again. He even held my hand as we were walking through the vineyards one evening. But we had become strangers of sorts. We changed into pajamas behind closed doors in the bathroom and slept chastely in the same bed.

47

IT WAS HIGH TIME FOR ME TO TRY to perfect my Spanish, and Bertrand left some money for the project and a request for Noelle to go with me to language school in Mexico when he died. I convinced Emily Lutken, my friend who was the Family Practitioner on the project, to miss some prime days of fishing and come with us too. We went to Morelia for a week in September and became schoolgirls again with our books and backpacks.

Morelia and Patzcuaro were the two major towns in the Mexican state of Michoacan. They were both colonial and only a thirty minute drive from each other, but they were totally different. Patzcuaro was the original Purepechan capital. The Spanish, when they arrived, changed the capitol to Morelia and built an impressive city as competition, but the indigenous people paid no mind. So Morelia had an austere Spanish quality, and Patzcuaro remained the colorful center of commerce.

The language school in Morelia was near the cathedral and was made up of simple classrooms around a courtyard draped in hot pink bouganvillas. I was put in an advanced class by myself, and my head ached from the hours of one-on-one conversation at the end of the day; I was jealous when I could hear Emily and Noelle laughing in the next room over. We were assigned loads of homework and barely had time to eat.

Emily and I got sick halfway through. We diagnosed ourselves as having Salmonella from the chicken in a restaurant that was too expensive to be very busy. We couldn't even leave our rooms until late afternoon when Noelle returned from class. She told us our teachers were quite amused when she said 'Las Doctoras estan infermas y el problema es el pollo.' We wrote a school report of what we did the day we missed school and made ourselves laugh until we cried. 'Mi estomago no esta bien. Voy al bano muchas, muchas veces. Vomito mucho. Tengo diarrhea tambien, diarrhea como agua. Ahora, tengo mucho dolor en mi cabeza y probablemente fievre. No es possible de caminar. Estaba en mi cama todo el dia o en el bano. Pienso que es el pollo malo. Nunca voy a comer pollo en el futuro.'

Later in the week, John came down to finish the paperwork and close on the clinic building. We all went to Patzcuaro for the weekend. Noelle and Emily both loved it there, and we pounded the streets practicing our Spanish. I found Poncha, introduced Noelle to her, and we all gave her twenty dollars. She looked a little more perplexed each time she saw me, but she had stopped offering napkins in exchange anymore.

We went to have blackberry Margaritas at La Basilica which had a parapet overlooking the stepped layers of ceramic tile that roofed the town. As I watched a cat crossing from house to house and a woman hanging out her laundry on the rooftops below, I wondered how we should proceed with the clinic. Emily had worked in the refugee camps in Afghanistan and Pakistan in the past, so I knew she had a grasp of what could be accomplished.

I asked her, "Do you think we should try to run a clinic or a hospital?"

"Do you have a good idea of what's out there for them now?"

"It's hard to tell. There are a lot of places that don't help that much because they are staffed with first year medical school graduates and don't have any medications."

John piped up, "The hospital Jim and I visited on the Purepechan mesa was pathetic. No heat, no medications, and a big picture of politicians at the opening ceremony on the wall."

"Maybe we should start with a clinic and see how that goes." I was feeling more practical and less ambitious as time went on. Emily nodded in agreement, "I think that's a good idea."

John was on a rant, "The Mexicans are adorable, but they're corrupt and they don't give a damn about the poor. The photo-op is more important..."

I interrupted him, "I don't think that's necessarily true. The doctors I saw in at the hospital in Morelia definitely cared and were working hard."

"Emily, Shut up!"

There was a moment of uncomfortable silence after John's outburst. I stayed angry and quiet for the rest of the night, but he didn't seem to notice.

We went to see the building that we had bought to become the clinic the next day. It had originally been a community college near Patzcuaro on the road to Morelia, but had functioned for only a few months. Century 21 got the listing, and we snapped it up quickly. It was on the top of a small hill, a half mile off the road, and consisted of six square one story rooms which stretched out horizontally. A big connecting porch ran the length of it. The combination of the gentle slope and the mountains in the distance made it feel serene and special up there. For the first time, I could visualize my dream coming true.

We had to measure the rooms from the outside because Willy still didn't have the keys. Willy had also arranged for a guardian to live on-site and protect the property, but he wasn't anywhere to be found. For months, John had been going on and on about Willy's incompetence, and I was beginning to agree with him.

I returned home with Emily and Noelle a day before John did. Emily and I sat together on the plane. She said she thought that since I was down to three dogs, I should look for a puppy when I got back. I was a sucker for puppies, so it didn't take much convincing.

I didn't have to look very far. The next weekend when I climbed the Battlerock, I felt I was being watched and found a starving dog with her eyes fixed on me from a quiet spot deep in the shadow under a rock. She looked to be a little less than a year old. I enticed her with food day after day, and it took more than a week before she would let me touch her. I brought her back to the house and the other dogs were not too bothered by her, so I decided to keep her. I named her Lucky. She was a true mixed breed; the only identifiable blood was Rottweiller. She killed some of our chickens at first, but responded to our reprimands once she was well fed and settled in.

I invited Emily and Jim to the farm for dinner on a Sunday night to come up with a plan for the clinic that would help the most people possible. By that time, my office basement was already full of equipment and supplies donated by the Cortez and Monticello hospitals. We talked about scope of care, staffing, equipment, formularies, and protocols.

Our conclusion was that the best idea would be to run a dependable clinic, with medicines on-site, five days a week staffed by a local team; a physician, nurse, outreach worker, social worker, accountant, and housekeeper. Specialists from the Unites States would then rotate down to do consultations and surgeries. The architectural plans for the conversion of the school into a clinic were drawn on blue graph paper with a ruler and pencil. We carefully counted the squares to match the feet of the room dimensions.

Emily's experiences in the refugee camps reassured me that our goals were realistic and our barriers far from insurmountable. Jim had a practical western streak and participated in planning our hospital renovation, so his knowledge of buildings and construction was vital. After a few hours, we had a finished product. John was out selling wine that night. I was relieved that he wasn't there because it made everything so much easier.

48

IT WAS A GLORIOUS FALL MORNING on the farm. The cottonwoods across the creek looked like a blazing fire at sunset yesterday, and the summer triangle was just leaving the night sky to be replaced by Orion and his dog Sirius who had the most prominent star of all in his collar. I never noticed the Dog Star before living out West; now I was mesmerized by the changing colors as it sparkled.

We poached eggs for breakfast and had them with buttered toast. The chickens were laying like crazy, but since Lucky had us down to six hens, our eggs were going to be sparse in the winter. We planned to hoard them while we could and put a night light in the henhouse, when the days got shorter, to convince the chickens that it was still summer.

The harvest was a couple of weeks away, so there was not much work to do. All the vines were still netted to keep the birds from eating the grapes. When I let the cat out, she went to sit underneath a spot in the third row and stared up with rapt attention. I walked over to release the bird in the net above her, who had found its way in and couldn't get out. When I held it in my hand, it looked like the same one I let out yesterday. The crop this year was outstanding; the grapes hung in heavy, tight bunches under the canopy of leaves.

I gathered up windfall apples from under the trees, used the bottom of my shirt to hold a quite a few of them, and fed them to the horses on the fence line. Wally insisted on biting his in two, so I was left with a sticky hand, from holding the other apple half under his mouth, as the juice from the first ran down his chin. There was a huge quince ripening on the tree we put in a three years ago. I was eager to see how it was going to taste.

Max and Jessie were sleeping in the sun, and Laura and Lucky were following me. Those two dogs loved each other from the start, and I wondered if it was because of the Rottweiller connection. It was good because Lucky kept Laura active, and Laura was unbelievably lazy. When I got back from work at the end of the day, the other dogs raced up the road to meet my car. When I got to the house, Laura didn't even stand up. She waited, with her tail wagging, for me to come to her to say hello. I decided to take the two of them for a walk with me on the Ute mountain.

I picked the biggest apple from the tree for lunch and ran back to the house and grabbed a pack, some water, and a handful of peanuts. I tied my tennis shoes to my belt and put on rubber boots to cross the creek. A month before, when I tripped on a rock and fell midstream, the dogs watched me incredulously before they bounded over. I didn't want to have a repeat performance today because the water was already pretty chilly.

It had been quite a while since I read Bruce Chatwin's book 'The Songlines', but the Aboriginal custom of naming the landmarks on a trail stuck in my mind both as a beautiful thought and a way to keep from getting lost. I crossed the creek by my golden rock, ducked under my arch of fallen cottonwood, passed my beehive tree, where Pancho stole honey and got stung standing in the bucket of the tractor last year. I crossed the barbed wire fence by standing on either side of my balancing rock, which spanned the bottom and wobbled when I stepped on it, then got to Rock Creek by way of my deer tree, that managed to survive the years with only two branches that looked like antlers. A little further up, I walked beside my flood destruction, where I found the piece of china, then finally, got to my favorite cave with round dark circles etched in the pink rock and a pack rat's nest on one side of it.

When I got to the cave, I saw a deer stand up, but he didn't run away like he should have. When he turned towards me and faced off the dogs. I saw that he was missing his left antler from an injury long ago, but more distressing than that, his hind leg was broken. Lucky and Laura began yipping at him in unearthly voices and chasing him around in circles. He couldn't move very far and limped awkwardly on his three legs, the other was hanging and useless. I yelled for them to stop, but they took no notice. I threw rocks and pieces of wood at them, but they kept on him.

At one point he fell, and they ran to him and pulled off hunks of hide and flesh. He groaned and managed to get back up, but the blood made them even wilder. I screamed and screamed until I could no longer hear myself screaming. I ran the half mile back to the hill above the creek and saw John already crossing it heading in my direction. I yelled for him to go back to the house and get the gun and sat on a rock with my ears covered sobbing until he got back.

The strangest part of the whole nightmare was that I had been carrying the premonition of it around with me for twenty years. During my residency in New York, I spent a lot of time at the Natural History Museum. While I was there, I was both repelled and attracted by 'Sambar and Wild Dogs' in the Asian mammals section. It drew me in every time. I would stand in front of it imagining how long it must take an animal, which looked the same as one of our deer, to be torn apart and killed by five snarling dogs. I also wondered why they put it together and kept it on display since so many children passed by. Interestingly, it never bothered the children half as much as it bothered me.

Some years later, I was reading the New York Times Book Review, and Ted Hughes had just released his book of poems based on Ovid's 'Metamorphosis'. They quoted from his poem Actaeon; and when I read it, it was the exact sequence of events that I had in my mind eye when I looked at 'Sambar and Wild Dogs' so many years before. I bought the book and memorized the poem, as ghastly as it was. We spent Christmas on the farm with friends from Santa Fe two years ago; and on Christmas Eve, we each picked our favorite piece of literature or poetry to read aloud. No one wanted to hear the end of Acteon, so I had to stop in the middle.

Ovid's story is about Actaeon who goes out with his hounds and friends to hunt deer. They have great success; and he decides there's been enough bloodshed for the day, so he stops the hunt and everyone starts for home. On his way back, he stumbles onto Diana bathing with her nymphs in a secluded pool. She changes him into a stag, so he can never tell anyone that he saw her naked. He is embarrassed to return to his castle, so he runs back to the woods and meets his hounds on the way. He is then torn apart by his own dogs and hears his friends calling his name over and over again to come and see this last biggest stag.

The incident definitely changed the way I felt about Lucky and Laura. And I knew there was no way they could understand why I didn't look at them, much less smile or touch them anymore. To make matters worse, a month later, both of them went on a chicken killing spree and killed the six hens we had left. There were headless bodies around every corner on the farm. I considered getting rid of Lucky because she was practically a wild dog. But I couldn't find a good home, didn't want to put her in a cage at the pound, and Laura loved her so much. She laid right next to her and groomed her all day like she did when she raised an orphan lamb a few years before. We had pictures of her with a lamb lying in the crook of her stomach and its head resting right across her back.

Poor Jessie and Max weren't much company for anybody anymore. Jessie had alway been nervous, and in her old age she had spells where she barked continuously outside our windows. Max, the Brittany, was more deaf than Beth before she died; and his eyes seemed to be going too, so it was even more difficult to communicate. I decided to keep things as they were for the time being, but it was with strong reservations.

49

I WENT BACK TO MEXICO BY MYSELF after Christmas. I needed to do some legal work with Paulina, take the plans to Willy, and had arranged to go out and see patients with Nancy in her truck. My office staff was so supportive of the Mexican project that they made me feel less guilty about all the time away; and after ten years, thanks to them, my practice ran like a well-oiled machine.

Since I was arriving in Mexico City on my own, Paulina suggested her bodyguards pick me up at the airport. I went through the door from customs, with trepidation, and peered into the crowd outside. Initially, I didn't see anyone who looked likely; but when I looked harder, I noticed a gruff-looking man holding a torn piece of cardboard with Emily misspelled in faint black ink. I walked over and introduced myself. There were two huge men dressed in dark clothes, and they spoke no English. Sadly, for my nerves, they didn't know how to smile either. I followed them to the car which was right outside. It was a big black Suburban with darkened windows. I got in the back, and they got in the front without speaking or turning around. There was a loud metallic sound that echoed in my heart as they locked everything down. We drove in silence. I thanked God when we arrived at my hotel.

The next day, Loli Creel came to have breakfast with me at the hotel and take me to the law offices for our meeting. She had a good amount of initiative for being only twenty-five; it had been her idea to ask Paulina for legal help. Her English was charming and perfect, her blonde hair was pulled back in a ponytail, and she was beautifully dressed. We ate nopales from cactus plants, which were cut in strips and looked and tasted like green beans, topped with melted cheese for breakfast and drove to the

Santa Fe district where the Creel offices were located. Her commitment to the project filled me with joy. She was passionate about doing something to help the indigenous people.

The law offices were in a high-rise building where the Security Guards took our identification at the door in exchange for a pass to enter. We met with Paulina and Luis, Loli's husband, in a well-appointed conference room where someone came by and asked if we wanted anything to drink every twenty minutes.

Paulina, who was also around twenty-five and spoke perfect English, had done a lot of work towards getting our tax free status in Mexico. There were literally books of official Operacion Michoacan papers with stamps and seals. I answered her questions, with Luis's help, as best I could and felt so fortunate to have her working with us. There was a relaxed dinner that night with people of all ages dropping by. The various dishes appeared in the center of the table at half hour intervals and the salsas and tortillas were in abundance.

The following day, I flew to Morelia and hired a driver to take me to Patzcuaro to get the plans to Willy. We met for a late lunch in the small plaza. He seemed to be distracted as I was explaining our primitive drawings of the clinic rooms, and he took them with him. Fortunately, I had made copies.

It felt liberating to be in Patzcuaro on my own speaking Spanish and scrounging for food. I ate fragrant, warm rolls from the bakery around the corner for breakfast, ripe mangos from the market at noon, and chicken mole or beef stew with corn dumplings for dinner around four in the afternoon.

There was also a modern cafe on the main plaza that I frequented, which served proper espresso instead of Nescafe. While I was sitting there one afternoon, an eight year old girl, clad in pink, from a neighboring table moved her chair and her strawberry cappuccino over to talk to me; her mother never even looked around. She told me her name was Lisette and politely asked mine. She seemed very excited about receiving gifts and kept pointing to toy-filled booths around the square. When I asked her what 'regalos' she got for Christmas, I thought my Spanish had faltered, because she said 'Nada'. She explained that the presents came on The Day of the Kings, tomorrow, and were brought in by foreign men riding elephants and lions. It was a real test of my Spanish. She kissed me good-bye on the cheek when her parents got up to leave.

I went with Nancy to the Purepechan villages the day afterwards. We stopped by the pharmacy, picked up medications and supplies, and followed a rutted road uphill for miles in her truck. The women were already gathered when we got to the top. The clinic was set up under a tent. It had two chairs, a primitive bedside table, and a cot which all wobbled on the uneven ground. The heavy cloth of the sides didn't even reach the dirt in most places. It was dark and incredibly cold.

The patients formed a line outside and patiently waited for us to raise the flap. We saw many things that were easy to resolve with medications and many things that weren't. Bronchitis, diarrhea, and urinary tract infections were easy; chest pain, loss of appetite, and seizures were not. I was exhausted at the end of the day and went to bed without supper; I was so eager to take aspirin for my headache and get under the covers to warm up that eating was way down on the priority list.

When I returned to America, I had lots of questions for Pancho about the Spanish I had heard. He shook his head when I told him my most pressing concern. I wanted to know how to say, "Es este un sequestro?" or "Is this a kidnapping?" in Spanish that was quick and easy to remember in a pinch.

50

THE SPRING OF 2006 WAS UPLIFTING. There had been good snowfall over the winter, so water was in abundance. On one of my walks up the Ute Mountain, a few years back, I had discovered a ground spring which ran out of a mossy bank to create a creek. It began to flow as soon as the snow started melting, and I went to drink from it every year to celebrate the warmer weather. I would lie on my stomach and hold my mouth up to the spongy moss: it was the most delicious water I had ever tasted. That year I brought some down in a jar for Pancho, and he agreed.

John and I were getting along so well that he came over to Monticello to see me one weekend when I was working. We hiked up a trail that I had found on Blue Mountain, which led to high meadows full of wild irises. We sat in the sun by a noisy brook and watched the butterflies. John looked as relaxed as I'd seen him in a while.

"Look at the yellow butterflies, they fly around purposefully until they find another that looks like them, then they spiral upwards close to each other in joy."

"We should never forget how lucky we were to have found each other. I was leaving for New York to start my residency in two months when I met you."

"I never forget how lucky I am to have you. We're a great team."

"We are, but sometimes relationships need some tending. We should take time to do things like this more often."

"I know. I feel so much better. I couldn't live without you, you know."

I knew and had resolved to stay, but it was a much lonelier marriage for me because there was still no physical contact. John's depression had vastly improved, but his focus was still on marketing the wine and the glamorous life it created. Durango, Dunton, Telluride, and Santa Fe were his highlights. Pancho and I remained devoted to the farm, so John and I were out of step with each other. Clarence Stash dropped for the first time in months to say hello, and John barely had time to speak to him. Before he left, he told me he thought John had really changed.

Christoph came to Dunton one weekend when John was away in California, so I went to stay overnight and explore the high country. The next day, when we went hiking, the water was pouring out of the hills and we were often up to our knees to get across the icy rivers. He was a thoughtful man who was fascinated by science and interested in new ideas. His family founded a chemical company, which had thrived and was a model of efficiency in Dusseldorf. He was generous with his fortune, and his financial support for Mexico was my anchor. I remember being disquieted that weekend by his impatience with the Dunton staff when they were being inefficient. I wondered how I was going to explain how Mexico functioned to a German, or whether I wanted to try to explain at all.

John came back from California determined that this was the year we were going to make the vineyard commercially viable. He had tasting room signs made for the canyon road with arrows pointing to our driveway, produced fliers for all the restaurants within a hundred mile radius, and put a vineyard vignette in every local travel brochure. I decided to buy a storage shed so that I could escape when the masses arrived. I placed it across the property, put in electricity, and outfitted it with a bed, a desk, a refrigerator, and an electric burner for tea. I could see the cars parking and leaving from my front door, and no one could see me.

That summer, I spent many hours reading in the intense heat there. The dogs would wander in and out panting, and the horses walked around it and poked their heads in from time to time. The gatherings at the house always lasted much longer than I anticipated. I was often left wishing that I had brought over more food.

The more guests who wandered in and around the property, the happier John was. He truly enjoyed telling them stories and delighting them with our wine. They didn't seem to add a lot to our bank account at first, but he was sure they would be the key to Sutcliffe Vineyard's success. The vineyard was just starting to bring in a little more money than it cost; and after years of hard work, I was much closer to paying off the mortgage on the farm.

I remained reclusive and saved my energies for medicine, not showing off. John took every opportunity to challenge my anti-social behavior. He showed vineyard guests every room of the house when I was napping, rushing to leave for the airport, and taking a bath upstairs.

51

FOUR MONTHS LATER, WILLY CALLED to say that he had made no progress with the clinic building.

"Emily, I'm sorry, but there is so much to do with paperwork and you know how many permits they need."

"I know, Willy, but we need to move forward."

"I also can't concentrate."

"What do you mean?"

"I'm having trouble in my marriage and all I can do is cry."

Needless to say, it didn't sound like much of an excuse to me. John, Jim Hanosh, and I took another trip to Patzcuaro because we knew that we had to replace him.

We found another contractor named Camerino through Victoria, an American, who owned the hotel where we now stayed. He had done the renovation there, and it was beautiful and solid. We pressed him to add us to the four other projects he was already doing, and he agreed. He confessed to me that his life was a mess in the first ten minutes, so I was happy to see that it didn't slow him down any.

Our last night, we had a celebratory dinner with Camerino and an architect from Mexico City who was a friend of Paulina's. After we had drinks and ordered food, the architect said gravely that Paulina had called him with a message for us an hour before. We had a new legal problem. The Creel lawyers found out that the federal government didn't allow any foreign doctors to work in Mexico. Camerino looked up after the statement was made and said it was funny how quickly the mood changed at the table from really happy to really upset.

This was the conversation I had with Paulina when I got home:

"I'm so sorry Emilia, but we had no idea this law existed until now."

"But we met with the Minister of Health in Morelia, and she thought everything was great."

"She probably doesn't know it exists either."

"But our whole plan is to bring foreign doctors to work in Mexico. Isn't there a way around it?"

"No, but one of the partners in our firm is really upset about it and is going to try to get the Constitution changed."

"How long will that take?"

"Well, we don't really think he's going to be successful; it's just to bring it to everyone's attention. But a change in the Constitution. I don't know—five years?"

"Any other way?"

"Well, you could try to get certified as a Mexican doctor."

"How long would that take?"

"Usually around two years."

"What would it involve? Would there be tests?"

"No, but they would want you to have a year of Social Service."

"This is Social Service!"

"I know; I'm sorry Emilia."

"This can't be the only way. I've worked in Mexico with American doctors. They have to be legal."

"No, we looked at all the medical philanthropy we could find. The agreements are all informal."

"Meaning?"

"Meaning if someone wants to shut you down they can, and we don't want that to happen to you. You could lose the building and any equipment you had…"

"Can I look into some of my groups and see if there's a loophole?"

"You can, but you won't find any. The Creel firm is pretty sure about it, and they advise you not to spend any more money until you have permission to practice here."

I emailed every organization from every source that I could find, and they were right. The only legal one was Doctors of the World, a splinter group of Doctors without Borders, who had stayed on in Chiapas after the Zapatista uprising.

I decided to do two things. I frantically started the certification process to become a Mexican physician, and I volunteered to work for Doctors of the World in Chiapas.

I took all my diplomas off the wall in my office and tore them out of their frames. The Mexican government wanted copies of diplomas from high school, college, medical school, and residency. They also needed copies of my birth certificate, state licenses, my residency curriculum translated into Spanish, and a letter from the Navajo Nation saying that I had performed Social Service. They required that each document be apostilled in the state of its origin. I learned that an Apostille was performed at the office of the Secretary of State, was one step above a notarization, and was commonly used in international affairs. I had to deal with six of them; North Carolina, where I went to boarding school, South Carolina, New York, Colorado, New Mexico, and Utah.

For quite a while, there was a lot of paper flying around; from me to all of the six states, from them to me, then from me to Mexico City. I went to 'Mailboxes' on a weekly basis. It was in a white strip mall on Main Street on the way out of town towards Durango. The parking lot had a bump going in that scraped my car on the bottom. The four people who worked there soon knew me by name.

The first papers I tried to send to Mexico City were by Federal Express, which interestingly only guaranteed them to the border. After repeating the entire round-robin process, I only used DHL and paid an outrageous price of sixty dollars an envelope.

Over the next few months, I also completed an on-line application three times to Doctors of the World and heard not a word back. In desperation, I sent a random email explaining my plight and got a sympathetic response from someone named Rebekah. I was sure that she quickly regretted it, because I pestered her on a weekly basis then decided to go see her in New York City.

We met in a bar on Fifth Avenue, and I begged her to let me work in Chiapas. She said they had a reliable crew who went down, didn't get freaked out, spoke Spanish, and were good doctors. They were cautious about newcomers from previous bad experiences. I promised that I would not get upset, was a good doctor, and stretched the truth about my Spanish skills. I convinced her to let me come for two weeks in June of the following year. In the back of my mind, I had the idea that if we couldn't work independently, we could possibly use them as an umbrella, but I needed to see how they functioned and whether they were interested first.

A few weeks before Christmas, I returned to Mailboxes to send Paulina and Loli a book and an ornament in appreciation for all the work that they had done. One of my new friends on duty was concerned and cautious.

"Where were these made?"

"What do you mean? I have no idea about the cross. Should I look at where the book was published?"

"Mexico is by far the hardest country to mail goods to. They won't receive anything made in China."

"I'm sure the ornament was made in China."

"You can try to write 'Made in the U.S.' on everything, but it might get confiscated in Customs." Thoughts of the equipment piled in my office basement flashed across my mind.

"It's a tin cross for a tree!"

"And that's the other thing, it's going to cost you ninety dollars to send them." I had bought them both for only twenty, but I paid it in defiance.

That night, I made a fire when I got home, curled up on the sofa with my Pendleton blanket and looked at my lists. I skipped 'What we've done so far' because I wasn't sure anymore.

The next steps:
  Getting the rest of the paperwork to the government.
  Going to work in Chiapas.

Keeping Camerino, the new contractor, on-board.

What seems impossible right now:
    Being allowed to work in the country.
    Crossing the border with the equipment.
    (especially if it's made in China).
    Explaining the delay to Christoph.

52

IN LATE JUNE OF 2006, I arrived in Altimirano, Chiapas. The road to get there from the airport circled through the hills. The driver spoke no English, and the four hour drive would have been beautiful had I not been so carsick. He let me off with my suitcase at the hospital, and I struggled to find the nun in charge because the patients scattered around didn't seem to understand my shy Spanish.

She took me through a locked gate into a compound, which consisted of several pistachio green buildings, a defunct looking garden, and an open brick kitchen. The dog inside, ironically named Mariposa, snarled at me when I put my hand down for her to sniff. One of the sisters was appointed to find some bedding and show me to my room. She was practically blind but refused to let me help her make my bed. I stood there useless and watched her feel for the corners and tuck the sheets.

The room was large with brick walls, high windows, and three single beds in a row, each with its own crucifix. The communal bathroom had pistachio walls, a primitive shower, and a toilet with the top worrisomely off. Toilet paper was nowhere to be found and would actually have seemed out of place.

I met the three doctors who were all named Antonio, which made it necessary to call them by their last names instead. No one spoke very much English, and their Mexico City slang was unintelligible to me. They hung out in the dining room which had the same green walls, a small refrigerator and a TV. I found an adjoining room with some medical books in Spanish and flipped through them until dinner.

We had quesadillas with corn tortillas and hot salsa followed by mangos and atole for dinner. It was messy peeling the mangoes by hand, but they were delicious. During the meal, the three Antonios joked about a gang of rapists from Guatemala pretending to be the messengers who came to wake you up when there was a C-section or a delivery. (There were no phones.) They knocked on the table and said 'Doctor, tengo una consultita.' When Antonio Delgado confirmed that I'd heard them correctly, he told me not to worry because the gang in town had only been raping men.

We heard a loud clap of thunder, so we took the dishes around the corner to the kitchen, thanked the nuns, and went to our rooms. Just after I got to my room, it poured rain and there was a blackout. I felt my way to the bathroom and cursed because I had forgotten to take napkins to use as toilet paper. I felt my way back to the bed and sat in the complete darkness. I listened to the hooting on the street and hoped that Mariposa was as fierce as she seemed.

In the morning I figured out how to reach my hand into the water in the back of the toilet to get it to flush. I had a cold shower and ate dry Raisin Bran for breakfast. Milk seemed to be as scarce as toilet paper.

The hospital was beautiful. A line of rooms followed a serpentine course with huge windows on both sides showing off flowers a big as your head. The floor had inlaid pieces of broken colorful marble, and it wound around ponds full of noisy frogs and exotic jungle plants. The patients and their families sat quietly on benches with their feet dusty and bare. The men wore hats, white shirts, and knee length white pants. The women had skirts with many brightly colored ribbons circling the bottom. They were gathered in front and wrapped round and round with a sash, so it took quite a bit of time for them to dress and undress. My wardrobe was woefully inadequate because I didn't anticipate the rain. I piled on three T-shirts each morning and still shivered most of the day.

On the second day, I did my first C-section with Delgado. Sister Ana, who looked as old as the hills, took an eternity to put in the spinal anesthesia so we could begin. There was nothing I liked better than operating; but when you did surgery for a living, you had many weird nightmares where things aren't quite right. I had to keep reassuring myself that everything was real; we were speaking Spanish, the instruments were all different, the scrub sink was gummed up with betadine, the patient was not going to suddenly get up and walk away in the middle of the operation.

I walked into town later that afternoon and called John from a pay phone in the broken-up cement square that served as the zocalo. The town had only one paved road, which was straight with impossibly high sidewalks on either side to avoid run-off rainwater. There were a few primitive shops along it, and the dirt roads that led from it into the jungle were strewn with garbage. I bought two mangos for snacks in the room.

It scared me to death in the first week when the velador pounded on my door and shouted 'Doctora, Doctora!' for a C-section in the middle of the night. I pulled on some jeans, quickly scanned the note he brought written by the doctor on-duty (in Spanish), and ran to the hospital. It was a serious case for both the mother and baby, but the gods were in our favor. Sister Ana got the spinal placed quickly, Sister Julieta managed to save the infant, and Delgado was a good surgical assistant. An hour later the patient was standing at the bedside and wanted to take a shower.

These were the toughest patients I had ever seen. The cribs all stayed empty on the pediatric ward because the families slept with their children on blankets on the floor. One night Delgado took me by the building where the patients' families stayed, and they were all preparing to sleep on the cement benches. I decided their backs must be made of iron just like their feet.

During my second week, four men came in carrying a man who had been electrocuted. There was no noise as they passed me at the entrance to the hospital. They each held an arm or a leg and ran in quiet synchrony as he was seizing.

I became accustomed to the routine in Chiapas much more quickly than I would have anticipated. I perfected the method of taking a cold shower, had lots of napkins stocked up for the bathroom, and didn't choke on the dry cereal for breakfast. I worked with Delgado during the day and read in the garden out back during the long lunch hour. After supper, I looked forward to the steaming metal jug of atole with milk powder and going to bed early so I could stop speaking Spanish. I had even befriended

Mariposa, but it took many treats. One day I watched the nearly-blind woman lovingly bathe her in the yard and couldn't recall ever bathing my dogs at home.

I was, however, neurotic about the jungle creeping into my room. There were stories of coral snakes trapped in the operating room, and I saw several patients with Chagas, which is a disease from a bedbug bite that makes your eye swell to the size of a baseball and eventually leads to death from heart failure. I first used my raincoat stuffed under the door of the bathroom to block the giant cockroaches that crawled around on the shower curtain, then I noticed there was an even bigger gap under the door to the outside.

I incessantly checked everything; my sheets, under the bed, my clothes. One morning, when I checked my shoes, the left one felt heavier, so I dropped it. A tiny green hand came over the edge of the black clog; I found a frog in there. He didn't want to come out when I took the shoe outside, so I used my pen to gently persuade him to leave fearing some poisonous variety.

A roommate came during the end of my stay. She was a new medical school graduate from Mexico City in her early twenties who had been forewarned and came armed with Raid. She would come out of the bathroom triumphant after a spraying session and say, 'Un otro animale esta muerto.' There were pools of liquid and dead cockroaches in every corner.

My last C-section happened on the night before I left . The patient was a 28 year old woman with her twelfth pregnancy who must have been laboring for days with a breech at home. When I finally got him back up out of her pelvis, he had pressure ulcers on his bottom.

That night, I hugged the Antonios goodbye and most of the sisters. The nuns asked when I was coming back, and it made me sad to realize that it might not happen any time in the near future because my project needed to take priority.

Antonio Delgado got up early the next morning to tell me goodbye again before my taxi arrived. He promised that he would take good care of the last C-section patient and stay in touch. We sat on the hospital steps and giggled about our adventures over the past two weeks. We laughed the hardest about how often we checked to see if there were any new patients at the hospital. The town was so boring there was nothing else to do. When the cab drove up, he gave me a big hug and said it had been an honor to work with me. It was a compliment from such a fantastic young doctor. We had become good friends, so I knew I would miss him. I was truthfully going to miss everything.

I did bring some friends home with me from Chiapas; I had at least fifty chiggers in my legs when I got back. The itching and eruptions went on for months. I kept my legs covered all summer.

53

WHEN I RETURNED TO THE FARM, I realized that I felt happier in Altimirano than I did at home. John was busy with vineyard guests and the two young winemakers on the weekends, and I was spending more and more time in the storage shed. He was out selling wine every night, and I was eating tuna fish and beans on my own with no one to talk to. I was so lonely that going to the office was the bright spot in my day.

I cornered John one afternoon and said, "I think we should look into therapists in the area. We could go together, you know."

"I'd rather die than go to a therapist."

"Don't you think you're being overly-dramatic?"

"No, I mean it. I'm smarter than any therapist. It would be a waste of time. Besides, by the time couples go to therapy, the writing's on the wall"

"Don't you think it would be worth giving it a shot even if the writing's on the wall?"

"We're doing fine. We had that problem when you left last year, but everyone goes through things like that if they've been married long enough." I guess it didn't seem as serious to him as it was to me.

"Well, I might go see someone."

I did look into it, but the medical community was so small that I knew everyone within a hundred mile radius and didn't want to drive further to talk to an unbiased stranger.

In the midst of everything else, my mother was very ill in South Carolina with pulmonary fibrosis and repetitive heart attacks. Over the summer, I kept taking emergency flights home to sit in various ICU's and stare at cardiac monitors. John was particularly unsympathetic.

The phone calls from my sister Callie made me wince because I knew they meant trouble. I was sitting with John, Pancho, and the winemakers in the tasting room one day when I got a particularly depressing call that Mom was in the ICU again with an unstable heart, and it reduced me to tears. John turned to me and said, "Your mother's been dying ever since I've known you."

I ran out of the room and straight up the Ute Mountain. After a half hour, I got to a spot with large smooth boulders where I often sat. I had marked an 'E' years ago with smaller rocks on the biggest one as a flag of sorts. I sat on it crying quietly, and my attention turned to the absolute silence on the mountain when the dogs weren't with me.

I heard a noise to the north and went further up the deer path to see what it was. A wild mare and her foal looked at me with interest, then galloped off into the distance. I was finally able to see them after all the years of pursuit. They were as exotic as I had imagined. She was about fourteen hands with a chestnut coat and black mane and tail totally tangled with brush. The colt stood proudly beside her; half her size, with a black mane that stuck straight up like a crew cut and the same burnished hide.

John was gone by the time I returned. He never apologized for his comment about my mother. He laughed and said it was true when I asked him about it the next day. He probably felt vindicated when her condition improved over the next few days.

I went to South Carolina at the end of August to take Mom from Gaffney to Charleston to see her great grandchildren one more time. I dreaded the four hour ride. During the trip I made with her immediately before, we had to stop in two emergency rooms for serious heart arrhythmias along the way; and I was only able to get her home again by pleading that I could take care of her since I was a doctor.

Fortunately, this time went without a hitch except that I noticed an irrationality in her conversation. We stayed for two days with my niece, who was Callie's oldest daughter, her husband, and her two children. I was sad to see that my impressions on the drive were correct; my mother had fairly severe confusion when she was out of her environment. Her alcohol consumption remained on par; and the second night after dinner, the conversation turned to inheritance in a light-hearted way.

Carrie, my niece, said, "What are you going to leave me? It sounds like it's all going to Joe." Joe was my brother.

"I don't know. What do you want? I could leave you the sideboard. It's one of the finest pieces of furniture from the plantation."

"Actually, I was only kidding. It's not something we should even be talking about right now." Carrie laughed.

I jokingly said, "Hey, I thought I was going to get the sideboard."

She looked at me and said, "But you have no children to pass things down to."

54

AFTER MY RETURN FROM MEXICO, there was absolutely no progress with the project. I dismissed using Doctors of the World as an umbrella organization because they wanted to pull back rather than expand in Mexico. All my papers were gathered, stamped, translated, and in the right place. It was the beginning of September, and we were impatient for an opinion. We hoped that the Creel firm could complete my certification a little sooner than expected and vouch for my years of Social Service. I signed the charts in Chiapas as simply 'Dra Emilia', so occasionally I mused about how much easier it would have been had we not gotten tangled up with lawyers in the first place.

Creel still advised against putting any money towards clinic renovations, and no one on the Board could imagine waiting two years to start. I couldn't imagine taking the time off to move to Mexico for a year to complete the Social Service requirement if that's what it came to. These were the emails that went back and forth:

Subject: Clinic in Patzcuaro
Cc: Paulina
Dear Loli,

Christoph has just told me that we'll have to move towards selling the clinic and forgetting the project if there are not completed permissions by the end of the year. I think it's fair, we've all waited long enough. I'm going to New York December 7th-15th and hope to catch up with Paulina. Has she changed her email address?

Lots of Love, Emily

Subject: Clinic in Patzcuaro
Cc: Paulina
Emily,

How have you been? How's John?

I talked to Carlos Creel and will talk to Paulina later this afternoon to organize a meeting for tomorrow morning.

We will talk about what we can really achieve before december and I will let you know as soon as we have an answer.

We understand everybodies frustration and we would not like this project to end this way. We will though tell you what we really believe we can do so you can discuss it with Cristoph and make a final decision.

I believe Paulina does have a new email, I will ask for it and email it to you as soon as I get it.

I will call you tomorrow with news about the meeting.

Un abrazo, Loli

Subject: Clinic in Patzcuaro
Hi Emilia!

How are you? I'm sorry I haven't written to you in such a long time. Is just that getting installed and doing all the school work has been overwhelming...

I understand the frustration, I haven't been able to follow up, but I would be devastated if this all comes to an end. I thought things were being taken care of in Mexico. I believe though, that if there is still a chance to go ahead with the project, an element for success is to hire someone that is devoted 100% to it. That person could then follow up on things on a daily basis and report to the rest of us.

btw this is my email
Muchos besos!! Paulina

Considering that Paulina had just started a program at Tufts, and Loli had just had a baby, their dedication was remarkable. Loli called the day after the Creel meeting and was excited to report that they'd found a way to fast-track my paperwork so that my certification would be completed by the end of the year. My attitude was reduced to: I'll believe it when I see it.

There was no 100% person for the project on the horizon except me. I had no money to pay anyone else, so I needed to be the one to follow up daily and report on progress. I resolved to not lose hope and to try to stay in touch with everybody.

John had a vineyard dinner on the farm while I was away in Charleston with my mother. It was a gala affair with a line of tables down the center of the orchard decked with white tablecloths, candles, and flowers, and it was catered with locally grown food. When I came back, I asked Pancho how it went and he said that he had to send his children home.

I asked why, and his eyes teared up when he explained that John had gotten drunk and was hanging all over the waitresses, pawing and kissing them, and saying how beautiful they were. It upset his twelve year old daughter and ten year old son because they couldn't understand why he did something like that when he was married to me. Pancho said John's behavior was so bad that he had no way of explaining it, so he told them to leave before it got worse; which inevitably it did.

I didn't know what to do, but I knew I had to do something; and then a disaster occurred.

My dogs had various deaths; Sam died, as perfectly as he had lived, in his sleep, Beth lost her muscles, Dusty, her ability to eat. Jessie's mind was the thing that failed her. She had always been a nervous dog, which seemed logical to me because she was so stupid. The world must be a terrifying place when you don't understand anything. When there was thunder, she would destroy wooden doors and eat through cat flaps to try to get inside. In her old age, she only wanted to be in the house, and it was not for our company. She would hide under the bed with her tail and hindquarters sticking out, all day, every day.

We couldn't keep her in at night because suddenly she would panic and come to the bedside for reassurance. So she was outside every night; repetitively barking, panting at the windows, and circling the house. Even with her sixteen years, I couldn't see putting her down solely for being crazy and annoying.

On the night before my forty-eighth birthday, I noticed an odd change in the way Lucky and Laura were treating her. I asked John about it, and he said I was imagining things. I was sleeping alone downstairs, in what used to be our bedroom; and I vaguely heard her at the windows for quite some time before I noticed there were other dogs involved. Suddenly I heard Laura and Lucky barking in the same way that they had with the deer. I ran outside and found they had been attacking her in the same way, and it was too late to save her. I called John, and we put her inside. He was too upset to do much of anything, so I sat with her in my lap for the rest of the night. I could feel her bleeding onto my legs, but she didn't seem to be in too much pain. I wanted her to at least feel protected and sheltered for a little while before she died.

I left for work on my birthday and asked John to take both Jessie and Lucky to the vet to be put down. I deliberated about Laura, but couldn't bring myself to do it. He called an hour later and said that he had shot both dogs, and they were taking them to the cave to bury them. Joann and Kierra had bought flowers and planned a birthday lunch. We went, and they were incredibly sweet and supportive, but I never stopped crying.

John was out selling wine when I got home that night; there was no present or even a card from him to be found. I went to look at the blood on the ground where he said he'd shot Lucky, then started scrubbing the blood stains from the floor of my house where Jessie had spent her last night. I couldn't even look at Laura. I put their food down, hugged Max, and ran back inside the house.

55

WE SEPARATED SOON AFTER MY BIRTHDAY in September of 2006. John found a house to rent from a friend in a town near-by, and I stayed on the farm. There was no use in confronting John about his behavior. I knew now, from experience, that even if he improved for a while, without a therapist in the picture, he would be back to the same antics in very little time. He had always said that he didn't deserve me, and now I agreed with him entirely.

I told him that I wanted a divorce and scheduled a meeting with a lawyer. He didn't want a divorce; but, other than that, we had no real disagreement between us. I asked him to come with me to see the lawyer, so we didn't have to hire two of them. It was fairly straightforward because the farm was paid for, and we had no other mutual debt to resolve. All we needed to do was split things down the middle.

I knew that I was doing the right thing, but the problem was that I didn't know what I was going to do after I did the right thing. I was already tired of people telling me to take it one day at a time or I would never survive. I needed to have some idea of what to do next, and it was impossible to think about it rationally. I couldn't leave the farm; I was sure it would kill me.

Max died soon after Jessie, which was fitting since they slept curled up together in the same tiny doghouse for twelve years. He was so deaf and blind by the end that he was killed by one of our regular Navajo customers who came to buy hay. They didn't see him as they were backing their loaded truck out of the hay barn, and he didn't hear or see them either. All the dogs were in the cave except Laura.

I moved all John's things to the tower. It was amazing how soothing the mindless task of rearranging things could be, until I hit something that caused a crying fit. I continued to put Laura in the house with me at night for protection, but she was on the other side of a door that protected me from her. I would never feel the same about her; and she watched me, every move I made, with pleading eyes. I hoped one day she would get used to it and give up; John too for that matter.

I tried, every moment of every day, to avoid being overly self-pitying or sentimental; but in my worst nightmares, I could never have fathomed how bad it was going to be.

My parents gave me pearls for my eighteenth birthday. They came in a dark brown leather case which folded up like an envelope and was lined with cream-colored silk. The pearls got thrown in with my other jewelry, but for thirty years the case had held carefully copied dictums for life on pieces of blue-bordered stationary. I couldn't remember the source and didn't note it in my studious eighteen year old hand, but they were as simple and wise as the 'Desiderata' that I memorized at sixteen and just as essential to me.

I read over them and realized there were three things that I should work hard to remember:

1. Don't be afraid to admit it when you've made a mistake. Let go of the self-satisfied idea that you were right about everything, break the semblance of order, and cut your losses. Life simply isn't ordered; and reality doesn't conform to our ideals and illusions, no matter how long we hold them.

2. Be wary of self-denial. Make sure the source of it is self-regard, not self-hatred. Don't justify your self-denial by judging yourself by superhuman standards. And remember it's self-indulgent to pretend you're Cinderella.

3. Don't be afraid of being alone; it's a leftover emotion from being a child. Don't forget that someone who can't be alone is someone who doesn't know he's grown up. Don't look to anyone else to establish your identity. Be your own master and face the future with courage and imagination.

One of my most-loved T.S. Eliot poems had a part that I copied and tucked in the mirror so I could read it every morning:

You must go through the way in which you are not.
And what you do not know is the only thing you know
And what you own is what you do not own
And where you are is where you are not...
In my end is my beginning.

56

I WAS ALONE ON COMB RIDGE in Utah with a drop so steep and continuous that it stopped the settlers from moving across the West for several months until they found a guide. I got up at six and left the house at seven. It was now only eight, so I had all day to get along the ridge to the cut for the San Juan River. I thought I might need it since there were only animal trails and many steep cliffs to negotiate. I had always wanted to go on this walk and had made it part of the way more than once. I hoped that today I could complete it.

For a change, I had lots of water, and no dogs to share it with. My raisin and peanut mixture rattled in its tupprware container in my backpack as I was walking; I kept turning around to see if something was behind me. I had to remember the songline here because there were not many ways through, and I didn't want to get lost on the way back. No one knew where I was. I told Pancho last night I was going hiking, but I didn't even give him a state for the location.

I resolved not to eat until I got there. I was never hungry anymore anyway. The extra weight from the water was probably balanced out by the amount of weight I had lost lately. I stopped to pile stones into cairns and move sticks to form arrows at places that seemed confusing.

The sky was the unfathomable deep blue color that I'd never seen anywhere but here or anytime but the fall. The red rocks shimmered in front of it from the sunlight. The deer path was good, but hard to pick up on the other side of the rocks. After two hours I stopped for a water break and watched a bright green lizard sunning himself on a rock below me. He seemed so content and uncomplicated.

After four hours, I could actually see the cliff edge where the San Juan ran through; and five hours into it, I was where I wanted to be. The vista was exactly the one I had anticipated. It looked like a mini-Grand Canyon, and I had it all to myself. The river was still majestic from this height, and it snaked around the stepped sides of the rock in a ribbon of rippled light. The cottonwoods on its banks had a few yellow leaves left, and there were patches of bright green cheet grass on both sides.

As I was eating my peanuts, a raven flew by, looked intently, then circled around to land on a rock close by. I stayed very still at first; but when I realized he wasn't shy of me, I tried to throw him peanuts and he couldn't have been less interested. We sat together for a while and watched the river; and as he left, he turned sideways in the air and called goodbye.

Maybe it was Bertrand.

I found my way back fairly easily because I was so careful going out, but I was tired from the nine hours when I got back to the car. Facing home alone had not been easy. I hoped I would be exhausted enough to actually sleep tonight.

I drove into my lonely farm, fed Laura, and sat on the porch to watch her eat. I warmed up some beans and made toast for myself. I realized I hadn't uttered a single word out loud all day.

57

ON A CRISP FALL DAY IN OCTOBER, just short of our twenty-second anniversary, John and I went to see the lawyer together. We were so kind to each other during the meeting that the lawyer asked if we'd thought about counseling because we were the most amiable divorcing couple he'd ever seen. John laughed. I didn't even smile and pressed to continue with the business at hand. It was the worst morning of my life. We hugged outside the office, said we would always love each other, and drove away in separate cars.

I went back to the farm and ran inside the house to make myself a cup of tea and try to calm down. As I was waiting for the water to boil, I turned on my computer and saw emails from Loli and Paulina in the Inbox.

Subject: Great News

Cc: Paulina

Hi Emily

How are you? I hope you had a great weekend.

We've got great news for you! On wednesday we will receive your studies revalidation. Paulina correct me if I am wrong but I believe this means Emily will be able to work in Mexico as a doctor now?

Emily I just got this piece of news from Carlos del Rio and I was so excited to let you know that I did not ask for the details but I will get back to you with more information.

Also I wanted to thank Paulina because this is all her doing. She is totally responsible for this amazing news. I hope you can meet each other in NY as you had wanted. I'll get back to you with more.

Un abrazo, Loli

Subject: Hola!

Emily,

Hi! I haven't heard from you since my last email so I assume you are not home.

Excellent news, we are obtaining your certification on Wednesday. Please call as soon as you get back.

Besos!

Paulina

About a week later I received this unsolicited email from Antonio Delgado in Chiapas. He'd written back to let me know that my last C-section patient was discharged the day after I left, but I hadn't heard from him since August. Life never ceased to amaze me.

Hello Emily!!

this is Tonio from Hospital San Carlos. How are you? What about your medical proyect in Mexico?

I'm going to finish my medical service in Chiapas in January 2007, I would like to know if you have vacancies for your hospital in Morelia, I'm interested to be part of your proyect.

Please write me back. keep in touch.

Antonio Delgado

I enlisted him for January and immediately booked a flight to Patzcuaro to go find Camerino.

Camerino and I spent many hours putting everything together. He proved to be as practical as Willy was not. He hired a locksmith to come and open every door. We measured the space for all the interior rooms, hallways, doors, windows, toilets, and appliances; then painstakingly drew and labeled them in chalk on the floor. We discussed lights, outlets, heaters, and ventilation. He had great ideas about built-in sinks, desks, counters, and shelving. I even picked out all the paint colors.

He fired the useless guardian who had been there since we bought the place and said he could find a new one at half the price. We drew up plans for a guardian's house on-site which, amazingly, was only going to cost $6,000 to build. Camerino also planned to cover the cost of the guardian until the clinic was completed because one of his men needed to be there anyway to guard the lumber and equipment.

We still had tasks to complete the early evening of the last day. I went to his shop to pick out windows and doors; and we went back to the clinic one last time, before the light left the sky, to recheck the measurements and plans. That night he brought a contract by the hotel at nine o'clock. He explained every clause because I couldn't take the time to unravel the Spanish. We agreed, shook hands, and I signed it. I got up at three-thirty the next morning and took the early flight from Morelia home.

Now I had to come up with the money. My Board had lost faith; not so much in me as in the Mexican government; although, Christoph did mention that he wasn't as confident of me without John. I understood their frustration about the amount of time it had taken to get started and felt that I had to prove myself before I went to them for any more support. I had some money set aside from a house we sold immediately after the divorce. It wasn't even going to cover half the cost, so I went to the bank and wantonly arranged a note for the rest.

58

"IT LOOKS GREAT!" Antonio was talking about the clinic as we drove past it in the dark on the way to Patzcuaro. He had picked me up from the eight o'clock flight at the airport in Morelia, and we stopped for a beer and some tacos in town before the thirty minute drive home.

"Why are you laughing?"

"Did Camerino choose the colors?"

"No, I did. Why? What's wrong with the colors?"

"You're going to need sunglasses to look at the yellow outside, but I'm sure it will fade really fast in the sun."

"How yellow is it? I don't think the one I picked was that bright."

"Camerino must have changed it then."

"What about the ones on the inside?"

"I don't think the patients will be able to sit with that green in the waiting room very long - it will give them a headache. But that way it won't get too crowded, and they can always sit on the porches... The pink in the last room is nice."

"I thought the Purepechans liked bright colors."

"They're going to love it then!"

We were laughing so hard that we both had tears in our eyes.

I had never seen a yellow quite that bright. It was as bright as the yolks from my barnyard chickens' eggs. It made New York taxis seem dull. The good thing was, like New York taxis, you could see it from a long way off (possibly Morelia). I might have chosen the headache-green in the waiting room, it reminded me of Chiapas, but Camerino definitely took poetic license with the yellow.

I loved the poetic license he took with the $6000 guardian's house. I would have moved in if it hadn't been occupied and didn't have two poor roosters in small cages on the roof. As three horses trotted by so close that I could hop on them from the porch, I made a note to talk to Camerino about plans for the outside now that the inside was nearing completion.

The inside smelled like freshly cut pine from all the substantial shelves, desks, and cabinets. The beige-tile floor, which Camerino insisted on and I initially balked at because of money, made everything look new and clean. I actually liked the green color in the front. I was happy with the long hallway down the center and the flow of rooms on either side. And I adored the rose-colored classroom in the back. There was so much space that it was hard to imagine we would ever make use of it all. I couldn't remember what functions the various rooms served anymore. Antonio and Camerino had to keep reminding me; no, this is the lab, no, this is pathology, no, this is the room for the ultrasound machine.

It was very exciting, but it didn't feel like that overwhelming moment, I had seen on TV, when your dreams come true and you break down in tears of joy. The only thing that I was overwhelmed by was how much more there was to do.

Antonio and Camerino were the angels that made it all possible, and they did it with such grace. No obstacle was insurmountable, and everything was a little bit funny.

Camerino was a jewel. He radiated masculinity. He was muscular with a little bit of a belly and had a sexy smile with beautiful white teeth. He consistently did more than he said he was gong to do in the initial agreement without changing the price. He replaced the electrical box that was stolen during Willy's time and bricked the sides of our very deep well. I talked to him about fencing and a garden, and he offered to find someone to do it and donated all the plants himself. I was afraid to mention anything else for fear that he would add it to the list of things he was already doing for free.

Antonio was so effective at organization and diplomacy that it was hard for me to remember he was twenty-six. And he made me laugh so much that I was afraid I would get new wrinkles. After six months, he had already won the affection of so many people in Patzcuaro. He was fairly tall with big brown eyes, an innocent, handsome face, and was always smiling. He was the perfect representative for the clinic.

Every restaurant seemed to have a 'mother' who took special care of him, and he had found some fantastic places to eat. We ate toasted cheese tortas (sandwiches) with jalapenos, tomatoes, and avocados and slurped down banana-yogurt smoothies at a licuado shop, which was so noisy from the blenders that we had to yell sitting right next to each other at the counter. We savored chicken mole burritos with the rich sauce dripping down our arms. We stood drooling as the street vendor put three sauces on a shrimp burger in the zocalo and ran across his favorite taco stands around every corner.

I stayed at El Refugio, which was a hotel with ten rooms and three apartments. Antonio lived in one of the apartments in the back, so it was very convenient for both of us. My room had a fireplace and a cat that wandered in from time to time.

We had breakfast each morning at eight in a dining room with two sideboards, a silver service, and a big, brightly colored painting of the 'Day of the Dead' celebration. Then we plotted things out and made lists in the warm sunlight of the courtyard among the flowers and fountains. We went to the zocalo for strong coffee mid-morning, and there were endless meetings in the afternoon. At dinner, we would have a beer or two then go to bed early and start all over again the next day. While I was there, I searched the streets for Poncha, but couldn't find her. I gave Antonio a detailed description and twenty dollars before I left.

One evening, Antonio stopped to show me a tree in the hotel garden, which is called huelle de noche (the smell of the night). It had clusters of tiny white flowers that looked like stars. They opened only after dusk, and their perfume was heady, sweet, and strong enough to fill the courtyard. He turned on the fountain and showed me where he sat on his own in the dark thinking. I suddenly realized that he must be lonely in this new place and that he wasn't ashamed to admit it. It reminded me that we should all have the courage to be lonely at times.

59

I FLEW DIRECTLY FROM MEXICO TO SOUTH CAROLINA because my mother was much sicker. She now had a rapidly progressive dementia in addition to the problems with her lungs and heart. We had placed her in an assisted living facility called Magnolias in Gaffney. My father was still at home, but neither of my parents understood what was going on. All they knew was that they weren't happy about it.

I walked up the sidewalk flanked by friendly residents in rocking chairs and asked about my mother's room inside. It seemed like a nice enough place. There was floral wallpaper, a sunny dining room, and a room with brown la-zee-boys clustered around a flat-screen TV. I walked into her room and found her there alone. I kissed her hello and sat down. She stared at me, smiled vacantly for a few minutes, then had a fit of concentration and said, "Melanie."

Seeing her displaced at Magnolias was hard, and it was especially unsettling that she didn't remember what she had named me. Of course, I assumed that she recognized me. I could have been wrong.

It was either uncanny that both of my parents became demented at the same time, or it meant that there was only so much abuse from alcohol and cigarettes that a body could take. If it was the alcohol, then their thresholds must have been the same. Whatever the cause, the end result was that they were impossible to deal with. We couldn't explain anything to either of them, they were miserable apart, and they were not at all passive.

I stopped to speak with the head nurse on my last day there.

"You realize my father is demented too."

"Yes, he can never find her room or his car in the parking lot. Do you think he should be driving?"

"No, but we're not up for that battle yet. I drove behind him yesterday, and his basic skills seem okay. And we haven't heard of him getting lost. I'm glad he's lived here all his life."

"We'll watch out for him too. I know it must be hard to live so far away."

"Thanks, at least Joe's close by. I just wanted to make sure you understand that there's no way that he could take care of her at home; no matter how much he wants her there."

"I'll remind all the nurses. I'm pretty sure they know anyway."

"He can be pretty insistent and domineering."

"We're used to dealing with that around here." I gave the nurse a hug and waved good-bye to the friendly porch crowd. My mother's window looked dark when I located it from the outside of the building.

I flew back to the farm. We had a new living arrangement after the divorce. John was in the tower, and I was in the main house. We both knew that it couldn't last, but we were at a loss for what came next.

John was relieved, and I was stifled. He walked round and round the house talking on his cellphone and brought me a cup of tea most mornings. I was thankful that I was still sleeping upstairs. Sometimes I got up to talk to him, and sometimes I didn't.

His most annoying habit was to continue to introduce me as his wife to the visitors who came to the vineyard. I was too embarrassed to correct him in front of them; and when I reminded him later, he said he kept forgetting. It negated everything I had gone through to get the divorce.

I knew I needed to leave, but I didn't know where to go. John had to stay with the farm and vineyard; it was now his livelihood. But my practice was my livelihood too, and it was based in Cortez. I couldn't imagine leaving all my patients behind, but my mental health was slipping the longer I stayed.

My mother was so sick that I knew I should probably move back to the South. I was developing a phobia of my sister's phone calls because I felt so helpless and frustrated in Colorado every time there was a crisis. I was so neurotic that I heard my cellphone ringing constantly even when it wasn't.

Katrin, Christoph's wife, took me out to lunch in Cortez before the Dunton crowd left in early September. She said that when she divorced her first husband, the most helpful advice she received was to try to get a clear picture of where you wanted to be then work towards it. I couldn't picture anything. My soul lived in and around that farm. Would it die if I moved? Would it stay there? Would it eventually come with me?

60

I CLEANED UP MY KITCHEN GARDEN in the fall and wondered if I was even going to be there to reap the benefit the next spring. It was soothing work. I pulled up the tomatoes, peppers, eggplants, and squash and put them in the pen for the chickens. I cut back the herbs and mulched them with straw. I was spreading horse manure in the strawberry bed when my cellphone rang. I looked down and winced when I saw it was Callie.

"He's got her!" She was laughing. I assumed 'he' meant Daddy.

"What do you mean he's got her?"

"He went right to Magnolias and took her."

"He couldn't. They have security, and I talked to the head nurse before I left. They wouldn't let him take her."

"They walked right out the front, got in the car, and left before anyone noticed."

Now I was laughing too. I couldn't believe my father had managed to kidnap my mother from assisted living.

"Well, someone needs to go to the house, pick her up, and take her back."

"They've locked all the doors and aren't answering the phone."

"And I'm sure they're smoking and have drinks poured." Why did I always sound like such a moralizing prude? Why shouldn't they be smoking and drinking at this point?

"What do you think we should do, Emily?"

"Leave them for a few days?"

"She'll get really sick without her medications."

"She's already really sick. Let's at least leave them for a day or two…"

My mother was barely conscious by the time that it worried my father enough to take her back. I booked a flight home and found a job in Charleston. I arranged an interview with the head of the Ob/Gyn Department at the Medical University who remembered me as a student. It was perfect timing because he needed someone to head up three clinics that cared for the undocumented population in the area. I agreed to start in January.

When I was in a positive mood, being on faculty and using Spanish every day sounded exciting. I found a perfect place to live; a carriage house, more like a doll house in scale, behind one of the oldest homes in the Historic District. Things fell into place like the pieces in an easy puzzle, but my heart wasn't in it. Mercifully, the university planned to give me a week every two months to go to Mexico.

My progress with Mexico happened, as usual, in fits and starts. The clinic building was entirely completed, but all the equipment that we needed to start seeing patients was in my office basement on the American side of the border. Antonio called when I got back to Colorado and went over the things he had done.

"I interviewed and hired our team. They're all on stand-by waiting for us to give them a date. I made an affiliation with the local hospital, so we can operate and admit medical patients there. I found a good lab for our patients to use in town and negotiated a discount rate. And there's a big pharmacy with good prices near-by, so we can stock ours when we're ready."

"Great, so as soon as we get the equipment across the border, we can start."

"I don't have good news there."

"Have you talked to Paulina?"

"Yes, she put me in touch with someone in Importation."

"And?"

"And the authorities need photographs of each item, a detailed description in Spanish of its function, what materials it's made of, and what country it's manufactured in. They need letters from each hospital or clinic that donated items with detailed lists of what they gave, and all our legal papers and licenses in Mexico."

"That's going to take forever. How can we figure out what materials an ultrasound machine is made of?"

"I can concentrate on the paperwork if you can get me the photographs, where things were made, serial numbers, and hospital papers."

"It's going to take at least a month. We can't wait a month to start."

"It's going to take a lot longer than a month. They said when the papers are ready, they are delivered to the desk of the Minister of Health, where they usually sit for two months waiting for his approval, then they go to the state government where it takes at least six more weeks to get the final permission to cross."

"This is madness!"

"I know, the Creel firm is pretty upset about it."

"And they're going to try to either change the Constitution or fast track the papers."

"How did you know?" Antonio was laughing, then got serious as he dealt the last blow "There is another problem. We need to have the official license for the clinic in place here to get the permissions."

"So, let's get it right away."

"We can't get it until we start seeing patients."

"But we need the equipment across the border to see patients."

"And we can't get the equipment across without the license."

"I'm getting a headache. I think we should do the best we can to get the papers in order for the permission and have a fall-back plan to start in a month with no equipment and basic supplies from Morelia if there's no progress."

"Fall-back plans are always good here."

"I know."

Kierra and Joann went to work in their spare time photographing each item in the basement and examining the small print for serial numbers and 'made in somewhere' insignias. I drew up detailed lists and got in touch with each hospital administrator or clinic director, who had donated equipment. I printed form letters and drove to Monticello, Cortez, Durango, Telluride, Shiprock, and Ute Mountain for signatures. We sent everything in files via computers. At least I was spared Mailboxes and my car, the bumps in the parking lot.

My lists now functioned less for encouragement than clarity.

What we've done so far:
  Built the clinic.
  Hired the staff.
  Formed alliances with the local hospital and laboratory.
  Finalized formularies, listed needed supplies.
  I've certified as a Mexican physician.

The next steps:
  Getting the clinic licensed.
  Submitting paperwork for the border crossing.
  Doing more indigenous community outreach.
  Working on protocols and methods of keeping statistics.
  Deciding when to start to see patients.

What seems impossible right now:
  Getting everything across the border.
  Finding more funding to pay off the note.
  Disposing of all the donated equipment and supplies in my basement.

61

I STARED AT THE FAMILY PHOTOGRAPHS, the white porcelain Madonna, the simple wooden cross, and silver candlesticks on my mother's dresser and tried to put them together into a unified whole. A photograph of me, Callie, and Joe in striped outfits with pointed elves hats for Christmas caught my eye. Callie was ten, Joe, eight, and I was a fat baby of two; you could tell they were trying to keep me occupied.

Mom was breathing fast, but was awake and seemed to be relatively comfortable. The thoughtful Hospice nurse had left the bedroom so I could have some time alone with her and was down the hall watching television with my father.

My mother looked at me and smiled. Her smile was blank, but beatific. As time went on, there were moans and words, but the words were sparse and practically unintelligible. She fussed with the sheets, examined everything close to her with a look of utter perplexity, and sucked her fingers. I caressed her hand to try to comfort her, and she finally fell asleep.

The sun was warm through the window on my back. I closed my eyes and remembered our old split-level house. I walked myself through the door and up the five stairs to my room, which was wallpapered with yellow sunflowers. I walked back down, peeked in the kitchen with the red linoleum table and chairs, and left to tour the suburban neighborhood of modest brick and clapboard houses around a circular road. I named the families as I passed the houses; two of them belonged to my cousins. As I napped with her, I was entirely aware that it was the last bit of pleasant time I was going to have with my mother.

I had moved her home to die with Hospice. She hadn't been out of the hospital since Daddy took her from assisted living; and I couldn't bear the bruises on her arms from blood draws and intravenous lines, the intrusive beeping of the heart monitor, and the hissing of the oxygen any longer. We brought her back to my father, where she belonged, and they both seemed more at ease.

Her breathing became more laborious over the course of the day, but she had no pain or obvious anxiety. The next morning, she was in a coma and unresponsive. I steeled myself for whatever the process of her dying might bring. Callie was catering an important party in Charleston and couldn't make the trip to Gaffney for a couple of days. Joe lived in the same town, but couldn't come down the block because he was too emotionally exhausted. So, it was me, Daddy, and the Hospice nurses in attendance.

I clicked back into a doctor role with the nurses, but it broke my heart every time my confused father asked me why she wasn't waking up. My uncle and aunt dropped by. I told them she was sleeping and wondered what they thought of the loud respirations coming from her room. Daddy, in a moment of lucidity, told them she hadn't been awake all day.

I stayed until Daddy went to bed then decided to go to the Hampton Inn and get some sleep. I told the nurses to call me if she needed anything or when she was close to the end. I put my phone by the bed, like so many nights on call, took the call at five in the morning, and went to the house to watch her take her last breaths like a true professional. But underneath it all, I was not a professional; I was her daughter.

After she died, I tried to call my sister, but her phone was switched off. I tried to call my brother, but he was not answering on his cellphone or at home. I couldn't decide whether I should wake my father up to tell him or just call the undertakers and have them remove her from the house. I finally found my niece, Carrie, on her home phone and asked for her opinion. She thought I should tell him, so I went upstairs with trepidation to wake him and tell him she was dead. He rolled over facing away from me and started to cry, but didn't seem to want to get up, so I went back downstairs and called the funeral home. The men who came to get her were from central-casting with their grim faces and black suits. I hugged the hospice nurse goodbye and sat by myself after they took her away. I rocked back and forth to comfort myself as I cried. I felt so completely alone.

Daddy eventually came downstairs and didn't remember she had died, so I had to tell him all over again. This happened so many times during the day that I was finally inured to it. But even if he couldn't retain it on an intellectual level, I felt he must have known it on a spiritual level, because he kept standing at the door of her room and looking at the empty bed.

Joe eventually materialized, and the two of us went to the funeral home to make the arrangements. Their overly large rooms were sterile with gleaming reproduction furniture. We thumbed through books of urns, chose a simple one, and opted for a memorial book with the least offensive sentimentality on the front. During our discussion, the funeral director felt free to have an interlude about finding the path to Jesus.

Callie and her family arrived from Charleston the next day. We searched the drawers of the old mahogany desk for the sequence of hymns Mother wanted, took them to the church, and planned the funeral. Food started arriving at my parents' house from all over town, and we piled it on the dining room table. We spent hours looking at old photographs and put the best ones in rows on the sideboard. It was comforting to remember her from the pictures; I was desperate to replace my memory of her at the end.

My father didn't go to the funeral. I was shocked to watch him fork down the meatballs on a plate that someone made for him from the mountains of food; he seemed to have forgotten that he was vegetarian. But he definitely hadn't forgotten that he was a raving atheist. At the very mention of church there was an emphatic 'No'.

62

WE HIRED A COMPANION FOR DADDY during the day, disabled the car so he couldn't drive, and instructed her to help him cut down on his incessant smoking. His confusion had a positive side in that he always thought Mom had just gone out or was in the next room over. I hoped it would be easier to manage his care from South Carolina than it had been from Colorado. At the very least, it would be much less travel. Airplanes, lately, were more familiar than my home. A few days after the funeral, I flew to New York City.

I fell in love with New York the first time my parents took me there when I was sixteen. I was determined to live there someday; so when I was accepted into the New York Hospital Residency program, my dream came true. It totally lived up to my expectations during the four years, and I could still remember watching the skyline disappear from the car window as we drove away when they were finished. As illogical as it sounded, now I wanted to rent apartments in New York City and in Charleston and had negotiated to share the one in New York with Carrie and her family.

I stood outside a thirty story building on ninety-sixth street with the traffic roaring by on First Avenue waiting for the realtor. The outside was yellow brick; and the lobby, with its beige tiles, looked as inviting as a bathroom. She was a brusque, middle-aged, business woman with a bob haircut and a navy suit. When she heard I had just divorced, she was quick to tell me that there were no men in New York.

We looked at only four places before I found the apartment that I wanted. It was a one bedroom on the twenty-seventh floor of a new building on First Avenue and was illuminated by the light dancing off the East River below. I told her that I only had two days to get everything in order with the lease. After Mexico, the paperwork seemed like nursery school.

On my last day in the city, I took the elevator up to the apartment and sat on the floor of the empty room. I tried to picture the life I was constructing and had a little more luck than before. The place was so small that furnishing it would be easy. It had the feeling of an eerie, and I needed a nest above the world before entering it again.

I went back to Colorado and started getting organized to move. Leaving my medical practice and leaving the farm were like the nightmares you wake up from and are so relieved are not true. I was determined to get both done, but couldn't let my mind consider, for a second, the long term implications of departure.

I called Mayflower and started to pack. John wouldn't cooperate with splitting up the furniture, so I took only my family pieces. In truth, neither of us could bear the thought of breaking apart the house that we'd been so happy in. I took my piano, a few paintings and rugs, and all my books; forty boxes of them. The piled up boxes looked threatening when I came downstairs each morning.

Closing my practice after twelve years was equally hard, but there were many more people involved. Joann, Kierra, and I spent most of our last days crying with the patients and with each other over the up-coming changes. I was touched by how many patients broke down in tears, and I wept with all of them in a mixture of guilt and sadness.

The hospital in Cortez was unable to find anyone to take my place because solo practices were no longer popular. I decided to keep everything in the office as it was for a few months in the vain hope that someone would come through. If not, the town would be left without a gynecologist and the patients would have to drive an hour for care. Kierra and Joann would have to find new jobs; and I would need to find a place that was accessible for the patient charts, figure out where to store my equipment, and sell the house that I had converted into my office. The chance of someone filling the gap that I created by leaving town was looking more miniscule by the day.

I took Rilke's 'Book of Hours' with me on every trip, every walk, and even to the office in the last month we were open. I honestly think it saved my life.

God speaks to each of us as he makes us,
Then walks with us silently out of the night.

These are the words we dimly hear:

You, sent out beyond your recall,
Go to the limit of your longing.
Embody me.

Flare up like a flame
And make big spaces I can move in.

Let everything happen to you: beauty and terror.
Just keep going. No feeling is final.
Don't let yourself lose me.

Nearby is the country they call life.
You will know it from its seriousness.

Give me your hand.

—Rainer Maria Rilke

63

In late October, the permissions to cross the border with the equipment were nowhere in sight, so Antonio and I decided to put together two clinic rooms and start seeing patients. I flew to Mexico City and met Antonio, Paulina, Luis, and Loli at the elegant Creel office to review the accounting we needed and how our tax-free status worked. The next day, Antonio and I drove to Patzcuaro. Just as we were starting, he fumbled in his pocket and gave me a twenty dollar bill. I was puzzled until he told me that he hadn't been able to find Poncha.

The drive was glorious. The rainy season had been plentiful, so there were acres of pink cosmos, yellow daisies with red centers, and bright orange marigolds. We made endless lists of the things we needed to buy from chairs, desks, exam tables, and lights to chart folders, pens, and paper. We stumped each other for words on the more obscure things such as iodine, sutures, and surgical instruments and resorted to Spanglish descriptions of their functions.

I rented one of the apartments in the back of the hotel because I was staying for almost three weeks. It was the opposite end of the Chiapas spectrum. Not only did I have hot water, but French doors that opened onto a garden full of bougainvilleas with peacocks strolling underneath them and windows with the clay tiled roofs of the Basilica outside. The bedroom upstairs was so spacious that I eventually moved downstairs to the smaller one; preferring to nest like a mouse in a sofa.

It took a full week of trips back and forth to Morelia to get medications for the pharmacy, cleaning supplies, stethoscopes, and table paper. We went back to Walmart three times to find a water cooler that didn't leak and finally ended up fixing the third one ourselves at the clinic. We repeatedly tipped the unnecessary parking attendant and imitated him because of his enthusiasm when he wanted you to pull out: 'Salé! Salé! Salé!'

The same week, we sent the rest of our staff to the surrounding hills and mesas to let the communities know we were starting on Monday. We were still nervously getting the last minute things done at nine o'clock on Sunday night. Loli thought that when we started the clinic we would feel similar to the way she had felt when she jumped out of a airplane her first time parachuting, and she was right; my stomach was in knots. I was imagining lines of people. I was imagining crowds out front. I was imagining more patients than we could deal with.

It was a sunny morning on Monday. We had an internet connection set up at the clinic, so on the off-chance that I'd have a minute to spare, I brought my computer with me because I needed to complete my hospital credentials on-line for Charleston. Antonio and I set up in two offices across the hall so we could see each other. The new desks were small and empty, the exam tables had paper neatly folded across them, and the sinks had soap and towels to one side.

I had more than enough time to put the preliminary data into my laptop and looked across the hall every few minutes to see Antonio gazing into his. The first patient didn't arrive until noon.

Arminda, our Purepechan outreach worker, was indomitable. She eagerly announced that we had our first patient and watched us debate over who would see her. We decided to do it together. Her daughter Marta was our nurse. Her hair was pulled back with precision, and she wore a starched white uniform. She handed us the chart then ran to our stocked pharmacy so she could dispense any medications that might be needed.

That first day we had four patients, and the second day we had two. At the end of the second day, Wenceslau, who was originally scheduled to clean for four hours daily, came to ask me if he could work full-time. I explained that I didn't have enough money budgeted to pay him all day long, and he said he wanted to do it anyway, so he could be more a part of the team. For the days that followed, he cleaned the hallway and empty waiting room incessantly with a big smile.

At the end of the week, we'd seen a grand total of twelve patients. I understood it intellectually. The Purepechans had no idea who we were and didn't want to waste the time or money on transportation to come and find out. Emotionally though, there was this feeling of 'what have I done?' followed by 'I've built a clinic no one wants.'

We worked hard on infrastructure and protocols in our unexpected spare time. Camerino had delivered roses, gardenias, bougainvilleas, and fruit trees; so the budding garden in front in of the clinic was beautiful. I kept walking outside to the porch to see if any patients were wandering up the road.

Our numbers remained the same for the second and third weeks; but we made plans for more outreach, radio spots, and a bus and driver from a philanthropic educational group nearby. After three weeks in Mexico, I had settled in so thoroughly that I didn't want to leave; especially since I had so many depressing things to attend to in America. I planned to go back to Charleston and set up house on my own for the first time in two decades. I was then going to return to Colorado and drive my car across the country before Christmas. Mexico was going to fill in any gaps.

Time seemed to be in abundance after I returned. The absence of a place where I wanted to stop and think created a lot of freedom. I got my house in Charleston ready and went back to the West to find that I didn't have much to do if I couldn't sell my practice. So, over Thanksgiving, I decided to run the Mexican border with the more expendable equipment and supplies.

I enlisted the help of our twenty-six year old winemaker, David, who spoke decent Spanish. Pancho helped us load a pick-up truck camper to the ceiling with monitors, gloves, scopes, and bandages without an inch to spare; and we headed for Nuevo Laredo. I had some paperwork, but I knew that it wasn't the right paperwork. We pulled into the 'To Declare' line. They thumbed through the lists, asked some questions, and copied our Mexican Corporation papers. Then they opened the back, looked with disbelief, and quickly closed it. We sailed through in less than fifteen minutes. We drove for two days, crossing many states, to get to Patzcuaro, safely delivered the equipment, then turned around and went straight back again.

64

I LEFT THE FARM IN DECEMBER OF 2007. My Honda Civic was loaded up with last minute things and looked like a college student's car on the move. There was a Mexican lamp that rattled, a painting propped on the other side of the driver's seat, a blender, and a toaster oven. My medical books from the office were carefully piled around everything for support.

I drove past the pink sands of New Mexico, the grasslands of Texas, the Mississippi river, Memphis in the rain, and Nashville in the sun. I sang at the top of my lungs with Annie Lennox, the Cowboy Junkies, Sheryl Crow, and Tracy Chapman. I thought a lot. I cried a lot. I kept going over what my father told me when he took me to boarding school in North Carolina at age fifteen. He said I had no choice about where I was going, but I did have a choice about the journey there; and it could be pleasant or very unpleasant depending on what I decided.

I had no choice. I couldn't continue to live fourteen miles down a lonely road in a house beside my ex-husband who often burst into tears when he saw me. With John, my heart finally shut down to protect itself; but I did still love my farm, it had done nothing to hurt me.

As I dropped into Maggie Valley in the Appalachian Mountains at dusk on the third and last day of the drive, I remembered going there as a child. The Smokies looked green, gentle, familiar, and mysterious all at the same time. There were beautiful places everywhere. I told myself that it was going to be okay; I was coming home.

I got into Charleston at around eleven and was thankful that I had the foresight to set up the house a month earlier. As I fumbled with the key in the lock, I smelled the blossom from the tea olive bush beside the door; the sweet scent of tea olives were my mother's favorite thing about Charleston.

I carried my heavy suitcase upstairs, plonked it on the floor, washed my face, and brushed my teeth. I crawled into my new bed and didn't wake up until I heard the mockingbirds singing in the morning.

I took a mug of milky coffee out into the walled garden and sat among the red, pink, and white camellias. It felt amazingly warm in South Carolina after eighteen winters in the Four Corners. I went for a walk through the old, uneven streets under the arching live oak branches and marveled at the perfect antebellum houses.

When I got to the water and walked along the Battery, there was a dolphin close-by. He was heading down the river to the sea. He swam away smoothly, arching up for air at very regular intervals. I could hear him breaking the water as he moved. The sound was repetitive and soothing. I could hear it even after he was no longer in sight.

There were lots of good-byes; the saddest were with Pancho and his family, Joann and Kierra, Laura, who I had forgiven, and the horses. No one materialized to take over my practice, so I kept Kierra working to send out letters saying that the office had closed and to copy charts. Joann had already found another job.

Laura seemed so lonely after I'd gone that John continued to let her into the mudroom of the main house to sleep. He had decided to continue living in the tower; and at eleven years old, she had a hard time getting up the stairs to his bedroom on the second floor.

Ten days after I left, when he opened the door to let her out in the morning, he found her dead on her blanket. There was no apparent cause, and I wondered if somehow she knew that I had driven away for good that last time.

About a month after I left, John and Pancho found Handsome, John's horse, dead in the field. Pancho was superstitious and became convinced that everything on the farm was going to die without me. I reminded him just how old both those animals were, but he was so upset himself that he continued to make me feel guilty.

A few days after I got to Charleston, I came down with the flu. I was sick for so long that I got into a routine of dragging myself to work and coming home at night and getting straight into bed. On the weekends, I often stayed in bed all day in the hopes of a more rapid recovery. It was two months before I finally got well.

Charleston looked pretty from my second floor windows as I took aspirin, slurped soup, and soaked in the bath. I occasionally ventured out to pick variegated camellias and line them up in vases on the deep windowsills. At night I could hear the ships calling to each other at sea; in the mornings, church bells and birdsong.

As soon as I had the energy to go out, I spent time with Carrie, her three girls, and Butter, their Labrador. The house was frenetic, because all of the children were under four years old, but it was exactly what I needed. I started taking Butter to the beach in the mornings on the weekends and their oldest daughter, Caroline, out for ice creams.

65

IN MID FEBRUARY, CALLIE CALLED and asked me over for dinner to sample a bread salad with roast chicken that she planned to cook for a party the next week. I was sick of soup, so I eagerly accepted. It was delicious, but the conversation was less spontaneous and the atmosphere much more loaded with Callie and Tom, my brother-in-law, that night. We were sitting at their kitchen table after dinner, looking out at the harbor, when Tom said, "You need a drink." I remember wondering what else could possibly go wrong.

The issue was my parent's will. Since my father was demented, parts of it needed to go into effect. Apparently, it was hard to find; and when it was finally located, it was so bizarre that Tom had another lawyer look at it. The lawyer concluded that it was legitimate.

Tom and Callie broke the news that I had been disinherited. At first I was relieved that it was only that, only money and family property. But as I sat there registering their sympathy, I began to realize the implications of knowing my mother's dying wish had been to exclude me. I chose to believe that my father was too demented and disengaged to do anything but sign where she told him to four years ago, but I kept staring at their signatures and wondering what it meant.

My mother had never been easy to get along with, and I had tried my best not to cross her and to be a good daughter. She was an intellectual and infected me with her love of literature and science. But I seemed to do many things that displeased her in my adult years. She didn't like the fact that I had married John or left the South; and when John and I found out that we couldn't have children, she was distraught. John was distraught too, and doubly so, because it was a problem with him and not me.

I delivered hundreds of babies during my career and never let myself consider what it would have been like to have my own. I avoided even touching the newborns in the nursery for fear that it might make me sad. And for the most part, I wasn't sad about it. But when John started to doubt his accomplishments and the marriage began to unravel, I wondered if children might have been his missing ingredient or would have kept us together.

For my mother, my inability to give her the grandchildren that she wanted was unforgivable. I thought I was being practical and brave, she thought I was being selfish. She complained to everyone she knew about my childlessness and let me know that I would be punished by not inheriting the family heirlooms.

The vast majority of the inheritance was left to my brother and his children. Mom had also made no secret of her preference for my brother. He needed psychiatric help as a child, and she often told us that we were the problem, as his sisters, because the psychiatrist said he would have been more stable as an only child. When we were growing up, we were constantly reminded of how much higher his IQ was than ours. And when he wasn't successful as an adult, and we were, she admonished us when we referred to anything in our lives that might remind him of his failure.

A book called 'The Three Maria's' was written by three Portuguese feminists in the sixties, and they seemed to have known my mother or many like her: ... *our mother who possessed nothing, who was hoping for a boy-child through whom her ego might even the score and take its vengeance, and who on seeing the girl-child that she had given birth to felt only grief and guilt for having brought into the world a creature like unto herself, with rights worth less than nothing.* Now she had proved that I had rights worth less than nothing by leaving me nothing.

Callie and Tom promised to do everything in their power to get the will changed, but nothing was going to change the way it made me feel. Like most people, I spent much of my life seeking my parent's approval, and the will's contents meant that I had ultimately failed to get it. And there was no way to appeal my case or ask questions. The verdict was final.

66

THE INTERSTATE TRAFFIC ON THE WAY TO WORK in Charleston was daunting, and there were daily accidents on my half hour commute. For a month, I kept turning at the wrong intersections and getting lost.

"This place is still so hard for me to find." I was talking to Faye, the salt-of-the-earth midwife who ran the clinic before I was appointed.

"You're lucky there's a sign now. For the first two years there wasn't one." Her desk and the chairs in front were stacked with so many various papers, charts, and journals that there was nowhere in her office to sit.

"No sign?"

"No, the Medical University wouldn't even name it. It was too controversial."

"How did the patients find it?"

"Word gets around pretty fast. We've got a big contingent from Brazil now. How's your Portuguese?"

"Non-existent and my Spanish is far from perfect."

"Did they tell you not to mention exactly what you're doing when people ask downtown?"

"No."

"I'm usually pretty vague about it. If you're talking to the wrong people, they might get upset."

"I figured as much and told the woman at the political fundraiser last night that I worked in North Charleston because I liked it here."

"Did she laugh?"

"No, she nodded politely and walked away." We both smiled.

Understanding the way things worked in Charleston was second nature to anyone who had lived there very long. Charleston was divided into North Charleston and Downtown Charleston which was further divided into below Broad Street and the rest. In fact, there was a restaurant a little over the dividing line named S.N.O.B. or Slightly North of Broad.

I lived below Broad Street because it was so beautiful, but I always felt that I had more in common with the Mexicans who worked for the landscaping services than the people who lived in the houses. North Charleston was full of strip malls, parking lots, and new businesses. It was where most of the undocumented population lived. How they managed to maneuver the twelve lane roads, brash American stores, and restaurant chains, with what little English they spoke, was beyond me.

The clinic was in the back of a sad, grey, one-story office building next to Northwoods Mall. There was a maze of parking lots; and at the entrance to ours, there was a small, man-made lake with a plastic duck adrift. The University said that the inside had just been enlarged and refurbished, but the carpet in the waiting room was already stained and there was nothing on the walls; I was told later that it was for fear of theft. One of the few pictures in the clinic was a print of the Diego Rivera woman with the lilies that they rather touchingly moved to my new office.

I was working with three midwives and a bilingual support staff. The waiting room was full of pregnant women; the clinic made up a big part of the university deliveries. The patients' fees were calculated by carefully set rules. We met regularly with the people in charge of our billing.

Fortunately, I didn't have many patients to start with because everything was in a foreign language. The records were electronic, so I went from the computer, which I wasn't comfortable with, to medical Spanish, which I was even less comfortable with. I was proud that I usually didn't need a translator for the Spanish; the computer interface with the hospital was another story.

It didn't take long to figure out that my career had changed. My job was primarily to supervise prenatal care and provide administration. The patients were sent to the university for any surgeries, and they were done by the attending staff there. I sadly realized that typing skills were going to be much more useful than my surgical ones and signed up for a free computer course called learn-2-type. I had a picture of the correct finger placement and the keys next to the mouse on my desk.

Work took up the majority of my time. I left the house at seven and returned at six Monday through Friday. I tried to recreate my life as best I could at nights and on the weekends.

I had moved the exercise machine to Charleston, but was totally bored with it; and the only hill I could find was the bridge across the Cooper River. I opted for long walks on the beach in any kind of weather.

I enrolled in an advanced Berlitz Spanish class for two hours every Monday, so I didn't get home until nine that night. I missed Pancho terribly, but the patients in Charleston were much easier to understand. Even the Brazilians were easier than Pancho; I'm not sure what he was speaking.

I signed up for weekly piano lessons at the music conservatory and found a strict teacher who made me start the piece over every time I missed a note.

And I went to New York at every opportunity that became available. I combed the thrift stores for second-hand furniture for the apartment. I rolled dressers on dollies across First Avenue and carried chairs ten blocks back to the twenty-seventh floor. I feasted on Peruvian chicken and Indian food and went to the opera and ballet. I was looking at the fields of daffodils in Central Park in the early spring when I got a call from Antonio.

"Hello Emily!"

"Antonio, How's it going?"

"Really well. We're seeing more patients every day. It's up to fifty a week."

"That's great!"

"We have several who need surgeries. When can you and Jim come down?"

"I'll start to work on it and get back to you right away." After all my work with typing and computers, surgery was music to my ears.

67

"WHAT DID YOU PUT ON THE CUSTOMS FORM?" I was trying not to be nervous, but I had enough surgical instruments in my suitcase to do a hysterectomy, and there was no telling what John Patton, the Anesthesiologist, had in his. He told me he'd left it blank. I had answered mine fraudulently. I wondered which would be better or worse. His could catch their eye; mine could land me in jail.

I sidled back to Jim Hanosh and asked him what he did with his. "I left it blank. I didn't want to risk them finding my equipment and seeing that I lied about it." That really helped my nerves.

And then there was the button for the red or green light followed by the x-ray machine that they put everything through. My suitcase was going to look like Hannibal Lector's. What was I thinking?

They smiled and waved us all through. I was breathless when we saw Antonio on the other side. I later learned that John not only had the equipment he needed in his bag, but enough drugs to put out and paralyze at least eight patients.

Our surgery cases were routine, but we felt that the entire reputation of the clinic rested on how well the patients did, so Jim and I were nervous. The first thing we did on Sunday, our first full day in Mexico, was to go to the clinic. We put together two surgical sets and pulled gloves, sutures, catheters, and bandages from the supplies that we had brought across the border in November.

We then went to the Hospital Civil in Patzcuaro where we were going to be doing the surgeries. It was a two-story building around a central courtyard and was old, but sweet, with a rose garden out front and a huge purple bougainvillea in the shape of a cross that dominated the central area.

We took the surgical sets there to be sterilized and put them in a giant autoclave that looked like it was from the last century. We changed into scrubs and checked the equipment in the operating room. The lights were fairly dim, the anesthesia machine had a bag to squeeze for respirations, the cautery unit looked scary, and the table seemed functional. Since we weren't used to organizing ourselves at home, we kept trying to make sure, between the three of us, we hadn't forgotten anything major.

On Monday, all of us sat quietly for an early breakfast in the hotel dining room trying not to look at the skulls in the colorful Day of the Dead painting that took up the whole wall above one of the elaborate sideboards. We walked down the hill to the hospital, changed into scrubs again, and fumbled with the unfamiliar shoe covers, hats, and masks. I was reminded of Chiapas when I found that the staff bathroom had no toilet paper.

Our scrub nurse was an older woman with laugh lines around her eyes; the rest of her face was covered by the mask. Her name was Maria, and she was dynamite. I would repetitively ask for a 'cuchillo', and she would remind me that I was not having lunch; a surgical knife was a 'bisturi.'

The operations went smoothly; and they were not too lengthy, so John's hand didn't get tired from pumping the bag for anesthesia, The cautery unit functioned fairly well, and the instruments were decent. At around six o'clock in the afternoon, as we were finishing up the last case, we started to have a little trouble with the light. We laughed when we figured out that it was because the light outside was fading through the window. We hadn't realized how much the daylight was illuminating our operative field. We all hugged Maria at the end of the day, checked in on our patients, then sat on the plaza for dinner and Margaritas.

The rest of the week was much the same. The hospital seemed totally adequate for care, and the patients were the same tough breed that I saw in Chiapas. The hospital administrator didn't charge our patients for food or medications, so we tried to replace anything we used on the surgery days and put together gift bags of gloves, sutures, catheters, and gauze before we left.

During the week, I realized that I loved going out to my clinic to see patients more than anything else in the world. The old couples sitting quietly, the wide-eyed children, and the women in their black shawls in the waiting room were the thing that I was living for. The rest of my life was an effort. I put one foot in front of the other and hoped that my soul would catch up with my body and I would become a whole person again someday.

The clinic was running well, but the funding was still hit or miss. I was happy to be able to bring down a team to operate because surgery was something these patients could never have afforded otherwise. Surgeries in Mexico could cost up to two thousand dollars and were a cash-only deal. I had heard of some patients being held in the hospital for ransom after emergency Cesarean deliveries.

It only cost $100,000 a year for us to stay open and see patients. Jim Hanosh and I had put in $20,000 at the beginning of the year, and Christoph had agreed to help until December, but I needed other sources. Finding them was not my strong suit, but I knew that I couldn't continue to fund it myself when things got tight. And I still had the note for the renovation to resolve. After divorcing, moving, and changing jobs, I was running out of money.

68

IT WAS THE FIRST SATURDAY IN JUNE and a beautiful Charleston morning. I awoke at six, padded downstairs to make tea, put together a small plate of shortbreads and dark chocolate, and carried it all back up to my bed on a tray. I pulled poetry books from the cases in the bedroom, Eliot, Rilke, Dickinson, Oliver, and piled them around me so I didn't have to get up again. I read for an hour and watched the shadow of a tree dance on the wall in front as the sun came up behind it.

The clock eventually put me in motion because dogs were only allowed to run free on the beach until nine. I pulled on a bathing suit and shorts, grabbed a towel, and drove across the Ashley River Bridge to get Butter. She was so excited to see me that it was hard to keep her from barking and waking everyone in the house. She leapt into the car; and as we drove, she alternated between looking out, with her paws balanced between the seats in front, or laying her head on the back of my seat so that it was almost touching mine.

We went over endless bridges across marshes, inlets, and rivers then finally got to Sullivan's Island. I remembered to grab the black plastic bag from the glove compartment in case she pooped, and we set off towards the water. As soon as I could, I ditched my flip-flops under a log. Her joy was palpable as she ran into the surf. She splashed around and looked back at me for approval. It was so early that there were only a few people and dogs on the beach. When approached by other dogs, Butter played politely for a few minutes, but was not terribly interested. She was in her own world.

The sun glittered on the water in the distance, and the shallows left by the receding waves were a mirror for the birds, the dogs, and my feet. I left my shorts and the keys to the car above the highest water mark in the sand and waded into the water to sit with her. She was too afraid of me drowning to actually swim.

On the walk back, I could taste the salt on my lips and felt it pull my skin taut as it dried. My hair was stiff from it; I tucked it behind my ears. I spread the towel on the driver's seat because my bathing suit was still wet and tracked loads of sand in with my flip-flops. Meanwhile, Butter settled down wet and sandy on the back seat. I reminded myself to take the car in for a wash next week. Last time Caroline came out for an ice-cream, she commented on how dirty it was, and she was only three.

I added my piece of conch shell to the ragged collection, which took up the space where the CD's were supposed to go. I was fascinated with the luminous colors on the inside of them and the fact that they were the hermit crabs' adopted homes. We stopped and shared a Danish on the way back. I gave Butter the bigger half; she definitely burned more calories than I did on the beach.

I put her inside the gate and told her what a good dog she was, but she was already distracted from being home and went to the back door to peer in at her family. I walked into the house full of the noise of happy, morning children and had a cup of coffee.

I had a good friend named Quincy. I had known her for twenty years because she was like another sister to Callie. When I moved to Charleston, she had also just divorced, so we became each other's lay-therapists and confidantes. We sat on her porch, looking at Colonial Lake, and drank coffee in the mornings and gin and tonics in the early evenings. We talked about feelings and relationships, our childhoods and early disappointments, men and women.

I caught crabs with chicken necks off Callie's dock. We took Tom's boat to an island nearby where the pelicans raised their young. We swam in the ocean on incoming tides and bodysurfed the waves. We ate great food and drank great wine; I often came home late at night. There was a gardenia growing close to the fence in the garden of the house across the street. Under the cover of darkness, I took the flowers one by one to float in water on my bedside table. I loved waking up to their smell.

There were mockingbirds, cardinals, doves, and seagulls. There was a squirrel I heard cracking nuts on my windowsill at dawn. There were trees so full of pink flowers that it hurt your eyes. There were palmettos that sang in the wind and marsh grass that popped in the heat of the afternoon sun. But it was not enough. I didn't know why, but I knew I was only resting there.

Daddy continued to get worse with his dementia. When I went to see him in the spring, I was genuinely afraid that he didn't recognize me until he asked about John. I told him we were divorced, and he politely asked if we'd had any children.

Victoria, the companion, stayed with him during the day; but she had a young daughter, so couldn't be there at night. She had no luck with controlling his smoking, and he left the house to wander the neighborhood if his cigarettes were taken away.

In late June, Joe called to let me know that Daddy had burned down half of his house during the night. I had been worried enough about the situation so that the news came as no surprise. We were all eternally grateful that neither he nor the closest neighbors were injured.

No one knew what happened, and Daddy didn't remember, so no one will ever know. It appeared that after the fire started, one of mother's old oxygen tanks was ignited. It melted all the pictures on the wall and demolished the curtains. When questioned, Daddy said he put it out with cups of water. I couldn't imagine how an eighty-five year old man put out a fire, compounded by an oxygen tank explosion, that was burning down half the house, by himself with cups of water.

We decided to put him in Magnolias where he could be watched more carefully. Fortunately, Joe volunteered to be the one to do it.

69

MY FIRST REACTION WHEN I REALIZED I couldn't settle in Charleston was panic. When the sickness and exhaustion from leaving the farm subsided, I had no doubt that I needed to move again, but I also realized that it was going to be hard to tolerate more instability. My family thought it was a preposterous decision after only five months. I was quoted maxims about giving places a chance for at least a year. But I knew in my heart of hearts that more time spent was only more time wasted.

Even though the South was my childhood home, New York felt like a better fit to me. I loved the juxtaposition of the culture and the grittiness, and I was fascinated by the people from all over the world who lived there. With Daddy in Magnolias and Mom gone, there was not as much reason for me to live close-by. And the Northeast was still far closer to the South than the West.

At least, I already had the apartment. I began to prep mentally to live in two rooms on the twenty-seventh floor. I was going to have to add even more things to the trail of my world that I had loved and left behind. There was no room for my piano, my china cabinet, or my dressing table. Ironically, I needed to get rid of most of the things I'd moved across the country only a few months before.

I also needed to find work. I saw a job advertised for a Gynecologist at an Integrated Center in Manhattan. I was unsure what that meant, but I applied on-line anyway. I got in touch with colleagues from my residency who worked at Cornell-Columbia and NYU and asked about jobs in both places. I wanted to let the Medical University in Charleston know I was leaving as soon as possible, but only after I had something set up with a start date.

My mind kept circling around the fact that I had made a mistake; I had chosen the wrong place to live. But I knew that it was a necessary interlude. I found a psychiatrist who helped me tremendously, I reconnected with Quincy and my family, and I had been there for my parents when they needed me the most.

But who exactly was I? I was no longer anyone's wife or anyone's daughter. I had lived so many different places and known so many different people. I didn't fit in the South anymore and had abandoned my home in the West. I felt so formless that one of my favorite books by Kundera, 'The Incredible Lightness of Being', took on real meaning.

My core had became an adaptable spirit that kept some internal integrity, but needed no sense of permanence. I had become so different from the me of eight years ago that neither of my selves would have recognized each other on the street.

70

CHARLESTON USED THE COOPER RIVER BRIDGE on the weekends for inspirational views and exercise. I was one in a loose line of enthusiasts on bikes and on foot when my phone rang, and I stopped beside one of the cables to answer it.

"Emily, this is Mitchell. I want to buy your office in Cortez. There's a group who wants to do Integrated Care, and they think it'd be perfect for them."

I met Mitchell when he dropped by my office to chat right before I moved from Cortez; now I better understood his motives. Integrated Care certainly seemed to be a recurring theme. I wondered if it was Jung's Synchronicity or that it was simply becoming more popular.

"I just had it appraised a couple of months ago. Would you take that price?" I hadn't even put it on the market yet.

"Yes, I will."

"Do we need realtors?"

"No, I've got a license, so we can handle it ourselves."

"Can I add one major condition?"

"What is it?"

"That I can leave all the stuff in the basement for you to get rid of when I move out?"

"Sure."

"You may want to go look at it first."

"No, I can get it hauled away."

"It's a deal then."

In early July, Emily Lutken and I went to Mexico together. It was a time of many flights and much lost luggage. My bag didn't arrive because it was mistakenly sent to Colombia, South America. I went shopping for underwear and cosmetics on my first day in Patzcuaro, then for clothes and shoes on the second day. It was more than a month before I finally saw it again.

Together, Antonio, Emily, and I fine-tuned our primary care. The clinic had enough patients to keep all of us busy; and, in between, we organized the supplies, the pharmacy, and the statistics. The obstacles had changed from being shattering to being amusing. I decided that I was either becoming more successful or going native.

Emily was from Louisiana and spoke with a drawl that made mine seem Northern. On medical rounds in Shiprock, she was infallibly the one who would cut to the quick and politely ask the question that made the diagnosis clearer to the rest of us. She was an astute clinician and an avid reader. Her bookshelves were jammed with the myths and legends of every country.

When she told me that I had done a good job with the clinic, it was a real compliment. She was glad that we had spent the week focusing on our primary care.

"Everyone always wants to come to these countries and operate when it's often the basics that they're missing."

"I wanted to do both parts. I just thought that surgery was more important because they couldn't afford it. It was such a relief when the lawyers decided that all the other doctors could work under my credentials."

"Well, now you've got a clinic that provides good general care, and you can build on that and bring down the specialists when you need them."

"Why do you always have so much common sense?" I envied her experience in the refugee camps.

"Born and bred in the briar patch." She smiled and leaned back in her chair.

"The next thing is getting the stuff ready for the Board meeting. I'm still not sure how that's going to go."

I was headed directly from Mexico to Colorado to sell my office, store the equipment, and meet with the Board. Fortunately, Emily was coming with me to the Board meeting in Dunton.

"We'll get them interested again. You need to let them know how well things are going. We've got lots of pictures and numbers to show them."

I flew into Albuquerque, stayed overnight, and drove to Cortez in the morning. I hired help to move my office equipment into a storage shed, in the vain hope that it would make its way to Mexico some day. It was a relief to ignore the basement which was so full of donated medical supplies that you could hardly walk around it.

The closing went smoothly, and I went straight to the bank afterwards and used the money to pay off the note for the clinic renovation in Mexico. I was relieved to resolve the debt, but distressed at my office being torn apart. I left for Dunton without seeing Pancho, Joann, or Kierra because all I could do was cry. I had wisely planned before I came on this trip not to see John at all.

I stayed at Bella and David's guest house which was set in a grove of aspens. Dunton was just far away enough from the farm to feel removed and just familiar enough to feel comforting. We had a noisy dinner, and I was doing okay until we went hiking up Calico Ridge the next morning. It felt so natural to be back on a mountain that the sorrow of not living close-by was overwhelming. I nursed the lump in my throat and pushed myself even harder, but I asked myself every step what I had done.

Emily came up the next day for the meeting. I had carefully arranged a time that would work for everyone when I arrived two days before. Emily had helped me put together pictures, statistics, and progress reports; I had stapled sheets of graphics for everyone. Included in them was a projection of how much money we needed and a pointed plea for help with funding. I also needed signatures on the By-Laws which had taken me four months to complete with a lawyer in Charleston.

At the appointed hour, the only people sitting in the saloon were me, Emily and Christoph; Katrin and Annabelle weren't back from their ride, and Bella and David were in the hot springs. When everyone arrived a half an hour later, there was still a lot of milling around. There were boxes from Abercromibie and Fitch that Katrin couldn't wait to open, and Bella wandered over to the kitchen to ask the chef what was for dinner.

I went over our progress as best I could, and we made vague plans for some brochures and fund-raisers in the future. My biggest success was in getting all the signatures that I needed for the ByLaws. When the thirty minute meeting was over, I congratulated myself for asking for help and criticized myself because I had concluded it with nothing in hand. I had a shot of Dickel with Emily at the bar and wondered if I was ever going to get used to my role in all this.

71

WHEN I GOT BACK TO CHARLESTON, I realized how much more depressed the job was making me. My patients felt as adrift as the plastic duck on the lake in the parking lot. I was talking about my recent trip to Patzcuaro with a pregnant woman from Mexico when she broke down in tears.

She said that her mother was seriously ill, and she hadn't been able to return home to see her in Chihuahua for seven years. She was a single mother; and her oldest two children, of twelve and thirteen, were still in Mexico with her family. She hadn't seen them in seven years either. She calmed down when she said that now, at least, she could send money home every month to make sure they had books for school.

The more I could communicate, the more I found out about the sadness of their lives. Mothers from Mexico, Guatemala, and Ecuador left their children with grandmothers and didn't know when they were going to see them again. Thirty-five year olds hadn't been back to their country or seen their parents in fifteen years. When I tried to put myself in their shoes, faced with their choices, and confronted by their challenges, it was overwhelming. How could you choose between watching your children grow up or making sure they had enough to eat?

After only a week back in Charleston, I flew to New York for my job interview with The Center for Health and Healing that integrated Western and Eastern Medicine with care from physicians, acupuncturists, physical therapists, nutritionists, and other assorted practitioners. My bag didn't come with me, but I managed to find something in my apartment acceptable for the interview the next morning.

Their office was on Fifth Avenue between two of the most photographed places in Manhattan; the Empire State building and the Flatiron building. I walked into the marble lobby with trepidation and told the doorman that I was there for an interview. He looked at me, smiled, and said, "I know you're going to get the job."

I took the elevator up to the second floor and was taken aback by how serene and beautiful it was. The waiting room had comfortable sofas, panoramic views of Fifth Avenue, oriental rugs, healthy plants, and dark wooden surfaces. It was balanced, and I knew I needed balance. I decided that I wanted to work there.

The doctor in charge was as enthusiastic as the doorman when I met her. She introduced me to everyone as the new doctor coming on board and arranged an interview with her boss, who was the head of the Center, the following day. When I left, I told the doorman that I might get the job and he gave me a high five. I went straight to Banana Republic and bought a change of outfits because I had no faith that my suitcase would arrive by the next day.

The Head of the Center for Health and Healing had his primary office on the Upper East Side. It was a hot day, so I remember already being nervous and sweaty when I finally found it. He was decidedly more guarded than the staff at the Center when I met him.

"So, what's your experience with Integrated Medicine?"

I felt a jolt of panic, then composed myself, "I worked with the Native Americans for seventeen years in the Four Corners and now have a clinic for an indigenous population in Mexico."

"And what did you learn?"

"We worked alongside the Navajo medicine men and are trying to do the same with the traditional healers in Mexico." I was feeling less confident by the minute.

"Any specifics?"

I tried to look thoughtful.

He then said, "I have a feeling that they want to hire you because you look good and are nice, but that you don't know much about Integrated Medicine."

"I can learn."

"Okay, but it's going to take a lot of work."

"I know."

As I walked out of his office, I hoped that last comment meant I got the job. I was carrying sheaths of paper that he'd given me about Integrated Care, Functional Medicine, Food as Medicine, and Health Care without Toxic Waste.

I flew home the next day. My suitcase had never left Charleston, so I picked it up on my way back through. The first Monday after I returned, I got a call to ask about my start date. I decided to make it the beginning of October to give me plenty of time to fill out, yet again, the forms for hospital credentials and a medical license in New York. I still didn't have my final license for South Carolina yet.

72

I FELT EXTRAORDINARILY GUILTY about leaving the job in Charleston that I had started only seven months before. As soon as I got the confirmation call from New York, I scheduled an appointment with the Head of Ambulatory Services and the Chairman of the Department, so at least I could give them thirty days notice. Fortuitously, I had only a short term contract which I was not breaking by leaving.

We sat in the Chairman's office which was decorated in Charleston nautical style. They waited expectantly for me to begin.

"I've really enjoyed my time here, but I've decided to move to New York." I fidgeted in my chair,

"New York. Well that's quite a change. How soon would you be leaving?" Dr. Soper was the one who had to worry about replacing me.

"Actually, I wanted to go at the end of August, so I scheduled this meeting as soon as I could to give you thirty days notice."

"Is there anything we can do to make you stay?" Dr. Van Dorsten, the Chairman, had been very accommodating with all my trips to Mexico.

"No, I'm pretty sure it's what I want to do."

Both of them looked incredulous. Dr. Soper shook his head and said, "Why would you want to leave here and go to New York?"

There was a pause.

"There's a guy." I couldn't believe what I'd just said. It was like an evil genie had crept into my mouth.

"Oh, now we understand!" They both smiled and nodded slyly.

"Well, that's great news Emily, but we'll be sorry to lose you." Dr. Van Dorsten shook my hand.

I will never know why I was moved to fabricate a story to fill in that uncomfortable silence in the office. I deserved the month-long torture, which followed, of elaborating on a man in New York who didn't even exist. I wished that I had been assertive instead of using a pretend boyfriend as an excuse, but I never ceased to amaze myself when it came to female wiles. They seemed to be programed in genetically and were my ultimate weapon under stress because they usually worked so well.

It would only be a month before I had to move again, and it was an exhausting prospect. I had enough furniture to fill the rooms of a three story carriage house, and I needed to sell every piece of it except two armchairs and the bookcases. It was going to be a fire sale.

I called Mayflower, and they quoted me the same price to move to New York as it had been to move cross-country. To save money, I decided that I would pack for myself this time. So many of my possessions had been jettisoned that the smaller things were mostly books, so it wasn't such a daunting task. I started to collect boxes from the grocery store and pile them up in a corner of the dining room.

I had an idea one night when I was out with Tom and the boys for dinner. I asked my nephews, "How would you like to help me load and drive a U-Haul truck to New York the last weekend in August for a thousand dollars a piece?" Needless to say, they were more than willing, and Tom generously offered to cover the cost of their flights home. I was comforted that this time my family would be accompanying me on the move.

Through a friend of a friend, I found a woman in New Jersey who wanted to buy my car. My furniture was sold bit by bit to everyone I knew. I couldn't find anyone who had the slightest interest in my beloved piano, so I donated it to the music conservatory. Over the month, I disassembled the house slowly by packing two boxes a day.

My plan was to set up the apartment in New York, then head for Mexico for an extended period of time before starting work at the Center. Through Antonio, I found a boarding house in the Condesa District of Mexico City, which was well-known for its bookshops and cafes. It would be the final test of my Spanish and an opportunity to try to raise some funding in Mexico.

On the Saturday before I left the South, I drove four hours back and forth to see Daddy at Magnolias. He was in a room close to where Mother's had been and was sitting in a chair in the same dim light. I brought him some chocolate and pecan candies that absorbed all of his attention for a while. I thought he still knew who I was, but I wasn't sure because he didn't ask about John. I described what was going on in my life, and he seemed confused. I realized anyone would have been; it sounded confusing to me. I asked him if he missed home, and he said he didn't know where home was. At least we had that in common.

73

IT WAS THE SECOND DAY OF MY DRIVE up the East Coast. My car, once again, looked like a college student's. This time my stereo was on the back seat protected by assorted sheets and towels. I was keeping an eye on my nephews in the small U-Haul truck ahead. My whole life now fit into the back of that truck.

Miles called me from his cellphone, and we decided to take the next exit and stop at Subway for lunch. We moved everything from out of my car into the truck and broke the glass on one large painting in the parking lot. We tore apart a box, scooped up the pieces, and relayed most of them to the nearest garbage can.

At a pre-arranged meeting on the New Jersey Turnpike, I sold my car and piled into the U-Haul with the boys. I loved that car and waived good-bye as we left; more to my car than the woman who bought it. The U-Haul truck was only a two-seater. I sat on the floor in between my nephews because it felt good to stretch out my legs. They played some of their favorite hip-hop songs for me at top volume.

I marveled at their generation's thumb dexterity when Miles punched the address into Map-quest to find our best route to my apartment building, the Post Toscana, on First Avenue and Eighty-ninth Street. McKinnon did a masterful job of driving. Our only accident was when we brushed up against the mirror of a truck on the way. I sat on the floor enjoying the unusual perspective of the skyscrapers and the sculpture on Grand Central Station.

We were in perfect time for the elevator, which I reserved from two to four. Unloading was easy because Jeffrey, the doorman, helped us guard the truck; and there were only books, rugs, paintings, and the armchairs and bookcases to unload. We had to return the truck to a lot in the Bronx; but, again, Map-quest came to our aid.

The boys decided to wander the streets for a little while afterwards. I made tea and sat and stared at the boxes. I thought how much easier it would be if I didn't have to put all those books in alphabetical order again.

The windows in my apartment had a huge expanse of sky in them. A few clouds were scudding by, and the light changed dramatically as they passed the sun. The East River was deep blue; it's afternoon color. I couldn't wait to see the red band of the dawn out my windows in the morning and the delicate gold of the first sunlight hitting the water.

I had made reservations at the restaurant Balthazar to celebrate our arrival. The boys had been planning what food they were going to order for days. We were shown to a tiny table in the middle of the restaurant. It was humming with voices and the noise of plates and glasses. The muted light danced off the cutlery, our champagne bubbled nicely in its flutes, and the duck confit, roast chicken, and steak frites were every bit as delicious as they smelled. Miles, McKinnon, and I talked about life after college, politics, racism in the South, and Mexico. I watched the parade of people waiting to be seated, the waiters dancing around the crowd, and the silent figures in the paintings on the wall who stood guard night after night.

After dinner, the boys went out on the town, and I went home to bed. It was going to be hard to adjust to calling New York 'home'. I was already half-expecting the maids to knock on the door so they could clean the room in the morning.

The next day, Miles and McKinnon flew back to Charleston, and I spent the day unpacking. I watched the big boats glide quietly down the East River and wondered how I had moved from eighty acres, that I was intimately acquainted with, to a remote observation post on the twenty-seventh floor. I signed a three year contract with the hospital and felt relieved that I wouldn't have any choices to make for a while.

At dusk, I walked across the street to the Peruvian restaurant and picked up my favorite roast chicken and salsa. I put the last book by Zweig in the bookshelf at midnight.

74

I LEFT THE FOLLOWING DAY. My flight into Mexico City arrived around ten at night, so I decided to stay at the hotel I was familiar with in Polanco then move to the Condesa District the next day. My suitcase didn't arrive when my flight did; but by that time, I didn't expect it to. I had become happy with the basics; a bed, a shower, and soap to wash out my underwear.

In the middle of the night, I got a call from the lobby to come pick up my bag. When I asked why, they said that I needed to sign for it. When I got downstairs, there was no paper to be found. I grumpily lugged it back up to my room wondering if I had misunderstood the Spanish, but feeling fairly sure I hadn't.

I moved to my new neighborhood just in time for my fiftieth birthday the following weekend. My room in the boarding house was small and simple. It was dominated by a queen-sized bed, and there was a desk underneath a long window which overlooked the classrooms of an elementary school. The white-tiled bathroom was almost as big as the main room with a bathtub and closet.

I listened to the children's lessons in the mornings and studied Spanish. In the afternoons, I explored the streets venturing out a little further each day. My daytime meals were solitary affairs. I didn't mind because the food was good enough to deserve my undivided attention. At night, I often met Luis and Loli or other friends to discuss ideas for fundraising. We worked on grants, pamphlets, a new website, and a television presentation.

On the morning of my birthday, I met Loli and the support staff from Creel at my favorite cafe for breakfast. I ate nopales, eggs with mole, and an assortment of Mexican breads. They brought me beautiful flowers. We then went to see the artist who was designing our Mexican website at his eclectic house. He had a cake and candles for me there and a few more flowers.

Antonio and Arminda drove up from Patzcuaro, arrived around midday, and brought an even more elaborate arrangement of flowers. We went to an exhibit at the Museum of Anthropology and had a late lunch at a restaurant that Antonio thought had the best tacos al pastor in the city. The soft corn tacos with pork, cilantro, and a hint of pineapple were my new favorite food.

In the late afternoon, we went to Xochimilco and floated on a colorful boat in the canals around the city with Antonio's parents. There were boats which pulled up alongside ours with Mariachi serenades, beer, food, and flowers. Antonio's parents bought me everything there was on offer, including another bouquet.

When I went to sleep that night, it was in a room full of flowers. My stomach was full, and I was pleasantly tired. I was glad to have spent an important birthday with the people in Mexico who had helped make my dream a reality, but there were many moments of nostalgia. I missed getting a call from my parents. I missed John letting all six dogs into the house to tell me happy birthday. I missed going down to see the horses, the tomatoes from my garden, and the peaches from my orchard. I missed dinner at La Marmot with John and Bertrand at the end of the day.

In the morning, I tried to think about where exactly I was in my life without the overlay of sentimentality from the day before. I had lost almost everything that made up my identity: the people I was closest to, a sense of place, my job as I knew it, the animals I loved, and my material possessions. But my sense of purpose still remained, and it had compelled me to struggle to create one good thing as a result of my sadness. I had no control over the bad things that were happening to me, but I knew I could do something positive for someone else. And by doing what I wanted, I found a place that I could call home. I was no longer worried about my authenticity because in losing everything, I had found it.

During the second week in Mexico, I took a bus to Patzcuaro. The clinic was thriving. We now faced the problem of too many patients that I anticipated the October we started. We picked the fifteen poorest, sickest, and earliest to arrive to see each day. Arminda said the Purepechan were already spreading tales of our magic machines, and we didn't even have the big equipment there yet. We had started monthly health education classes in the rose colored room, and we had another office which served as a 'free box' and was full of donated clothes, food, toys, and appliances.

I saw patients for a week there. One afternoon, Arminda and Marta brought one of our surgical patients into my room. We had done a hysterectomy for large fibroids and heavy bleeding four months before. She was smiling from ear to ear as she carefully unwrapped her shawl which had beautiful bags that she had made for all of us inside. She spoke only Purepechan. I remember listening to the music of her language and the birds singing right outside my office window.

"She says that she'll never be able to thank you enough." Arminda was translating for me.

"Tell her that we were happy to be able to do it for her."

"She said that she thought she was going to die before, and there would be no one to take care of her children. She thought of selling her oxen to pay for the surgery after she saw the doctors in town, but her husband needed them for his farm work."

I smiled. She took my hand in hers, and she held it tightly.

"She says God bless you."

I spent the final week in Mexico City preparing for a television interview about the clinic. Antonio, Arminda, and I all had to talk for a few minutes. They were nervous, but I was beside myself because the station wanted even my part to be in Spanish. Antonio had helped me write it, but it needed to sound more erudite than my elementary conversation. I memorized it word for word, but it was easy to get lost, especially when I was nervous. And I had never been on TV before, so I was definitely nervous.

Antonio and Arminda drove up again at the end of the week, and we went to the station for the filming. I thanked God it wasn't live. I sat in the room outside murmuring to myself with notes scribbled on a piece of paper.

When it came time, I recited it like it was the song 'Frere Jacques' that I memorized when I was ten. It might have been easier had it been to music.

We all went to Cuernavaca with Antonio's family that night. We sat around a table outside in perfect weather and talked, ate, and drank until the sun went down. then lingered long afterwards. Arminda and I shared a room to sleep.

I woke up in the morning to the soft sounds of Arminda getting up. I looked over and could see her thick braid of hair as she bent over the bed to make it up. I heard her bare feet on the floor as she gathered her things and padded to the bathroom. It was the first time I had felt truly content in years.

I went over the lists in my mind. I didn't need the book anymore.

What we've done so far:
  Opened and licensed the clinic.
  Performed surgeries at the Hospital Civil.
  Established community trust.
  Provided patient education.
  Gathered statistics, assessed needs, identified goals.

The next steps:
  Getting the equipment across the border.
  Securing more funding.
  Organizing more participation from American physicians.
  Continuing to expand collaboration with Mexican physicians.

What seems impossible right now:
  Nothing.

AUTHOR'S NOTE

SINCE THIS BOOK WAS WRITTEN, Clinica Juchari has expanded its free services for the Purepechan people of the Lake Patzcuaro region, offering comprehensive care and integrating Western practices with traditional ones. Arminda and our local staff now do outreach to the local villages, providing medicine as well as classes on nutrition and health. As medical director, I assist with planning and visit several times a year as a specialist. All proceeds from this book will go to the clinic.

In 2010, Clinica Juchari became a subsidiary of Heartland Alliance for Human Needs and Human Rights. Heartland's mission is to improve the lives of the poor through housing, health care, jobs and economic opportunity, and justice.

http://www.heartlandalliance.org

CPSIA information can be obtained
at www.ICGtesting.com
Printed in the USA
LVOW12s2222180117

521459LV00001B/259/P